Let's GO!

Let's GO!

The Epistle to the Hebrews for Twenty-first-Century Christians

WARREN W. WIERSBE

CLC
PUBLICATIONS
Fort Washington, PA 19034

Published by CLC Publications

U.S.A.
P.O. Box 1449, Fort Washington, PA 19034

GREAT BRITAIN
51 The Dean, Alresford, Hants. SO24 9BJ

AUSTRALIA
P.O. Box 469, Kippa-Ring QLD 4021

NEW ZEALAND
10 MacArthur Street, Feilding

Printed in the United States of America
18 17 16 15 14 13 12 11 10 1 2 3 4 5 6

ISBN-13: 978-1-936143-07-8

Italicized words in Scripture quotes are the emphasis of the author.

Table of Contents

1

Why Hebrews?

It was a Saturday night and the high school auditorium was packed. I remember hearing Billy Graham preach at the Youth for Christ Rally. I didn't go forward at the invitation, and I didn't even raise my hand for prayer. But I remember putting my trust in Jesus Christ as my Savior and Lord. I always had been a faithful Sunday school pupil, and had even been confirmed in the church, but I had never been born again until that night. Many prayers offered by many people were answered.

There were several other teenagers converted that evening, and the adults who had sponsored the rally knew we needed follow-up instruction, so they started a Tuesday evening Bible class in the home of a gifted Bible teacher who could feed both the lambs and the sheep, and he had a way of shaking up my thinking.

The teacher felt led to teach the epistle to the Hebrews! Hebrews always seemed like one of the books of the Bible that only great theologians in high towers devoted their lives to studying in great depth. Here I was, sixteen years old, just a few weeks old in the Lord, and I was going to study Hebrews? Me? As shocking as that was to me, even more shocking was when I discovered that studying Hebrews was the best thing for me as a "baby" believer. Week by week, verse by verse, word by word, we were shepherded through the book. Many wonderful truths were beyond my grasp, but enough stayed with me to make a difference in my spiritual walk. Those hours in Hebrews instilled in me a lifelong appetite for God's Word. I've been feeding on Scripture ever since, and trying to feed others.

That was over sixty years ago. Ancient history. Now let's come up to date.

If we name the name of Christ, we cannot live any way we please and get away with it.

If the church today needs to understand and apply one book in the Bible, that book is the epistle to the Hebrews. We don't know who wrote it, but we do know who needs to read it: every Christian believer. It is a book for the baby believer, like I was, as well as for the mature believer. Christians who have been seduced by simplistic slogans and "success" theology and who are over-awed by religious celebrities don't put Jesus first in their lives, and glorifying Him is the last thing on their mind. When it becomes more important to sit in the glow of the latest Christian celebrity than to get to know Jesus better, a careful study of Hebrews will help you focus on Christ, who He is and what He has done. When church becomes tepid rather than transforming, it's time to turn to Hebrews with a fresh eye and an open heart.

If you are a preacher and have begun to count "converts" but never weigh them and turn the "shepherding" over to others, it's time to spend some time in this amazing book and get to know Christ all over again. And what about saints who neglect the Bible, who have lost their appetite for the heavenly manna? Why? Perhaps they have been seduced by the garbage from the dumpsters called "the secular media." And, alas, there are professed believers who lead double lives, confident they will get away with it.

There's no "bumper-sticker theology" in Hebrews. The writer serves meat and not skim milk. He mentions great people like Abraham, Sarah, Moses and Aaron, but the only "celebrity" in the book is Jesus Christ, the Son of God. A.W. Tozer used to remind us that it's difficult to get people to attend meetings where the only attraction is God. He should see the church today! The role model in the church today isn't Jesus; it's the latest movie or TV star, sports hero or musician. Our Lord would never have made a good American idol. "He had no beauty or majesty to attract us to him, nothing in his appearance that we should desire him. He was despised and rejected by men, a man of sorrows, and familiar with suffering" (Isa. 53:2–3). Hebrews glorifies Jesus Christ.

Hebrews is about believers maturing in the faith, growing up and acting like adults on a battleground and not like children on a playground. *Hebrews warns us that, if we name the name of Christ, we cannot live any way we please and get away with it.* "It is a dreadful thing to fall into the hands of the living God" (Heb. 10:31).

"But that's for unsaved people," the careless Christian argues.

The writer of Hebrews replies, "Read the previous verse: 'The Lord will judge His people.'" Who? "His people."

In the pages of Scripture, we meet some of these people whom God had to judge: Lot, who moved into Sodom and lost everything (including his wife) ended up living in a cave, getting drunk and committing incest. Moses lost his temper and saw the gates into the Holy Land slammed shut so that even his repeated prayers couldn't open them. Moses didn't get in until he came down from heaven with Elijah for our Lord's transfiguration (see Matt. 17:1–13). David committed adultery and cleverly plotted murder, but he ended up going to his baby's funeral, weeping over his own daughter who was raped as well as over the death of two of his ambitious sons. Samson had to have his own way ("Get that woman for me!") and in his spare time supported prostitutes, but he ended his life blind and bound, grinding grain like a slave. Yes, he climaxed his life by killing thousands of Israel's enemies, but no Christian father today encourages his son to be like Samson, unless it's in Samson's repentance.

"The Lord will judge his people." Hebrews 12 tells us how our loving Father disciplines His children in love, and if professed Christians who repeatedly rebel aren't disciplined by God, they simply don't belong to God's family. Hebrews 12:23 calls God "the judge of all," and Hebrews 13:4 says that "God will judge the adulterer and all the sexually immoral." No exceptions.

The aim of Hebrews is to help us become better Christians.

The consummate twentieth-century preacher Vance Havner used to say, "It's come to the place in our churches where, if you want to fellowship with anybody, you have to backslide." Knowing and obeying the epistle to the Hebrews is a good remedy for Christians who ignore the Bible and prayer, find excuses to stay home from church, practice a juvenile variety of worship and comfort themselves with the false confidence that they will end well.

Some people think that studying Hebrews is impossible—like trying to run a marathon with one leg in a cast. When I was in high school, I hated Mondays because it meant starting the day in phys ed class, running the outdoor obstacle course, regardless of the weather, and then diving into a lukewarm shower. Then we would try to dry off and get to the next class on time without catching cold as we ran between buildings. Please don't think that the book of Hebrews is like that. It may not always be easy or comfortable reading, but it wasn't written to make us comfortable. *It was written to make us conformable to Jesus Christ.*

The aim of Hebrews is to help us become better Christians, and anybody who doesn't want to be a better Christian probably isn't a Christian at all. The author calls his epistle "my word of exhortation" (Heb. 13:22) and uses the Greek word *paraclete* to describe his letter. It is translated "exhortation" and carries the meaning of encouragement, consolation and comfort. It is one of the names of the Holy Spirit, the comforter, the encourager, the one who helps us (see John 14:15–27). Maturing in the Christian life has never been easy any more than maturing in our physical, intellectual or emotional lives is easy. We can't help growing old, but we *can* help it if we don't grow up.

Believe me, if you come to Hebrews with a grateful heart, wanting to learn more of what it means to be like Christ, then your "Monday morning" experiences will be fewer and fewer, and you will thrive on the encouragement the writer shares with you.

Specifics about *Let's Go!*

This is not a detailed study on the book of Hebrews. Rather, it's an overview and a practical application of the book's important truths to the life and ministry of God's people today. For detailed studies, see the brief bibliography at the end of the book.

First, we review the ministry of Jesus Christ in heaven today, serving His people as high priest, intercessor and advocate. Unless we know what He is doing in heaven, we can never avail ourselves of His resources to do His will on earth.

We will then consider four major admonitions in this remarkable book: let's go in (Heb. 1–4), let's go on (Heb. 5–6), let's go up (Heb. 7–10) and let's go out (Heb. 11–13). There are fourteen "let us" statements in Hebrews, but these four admonitions pretty well summarize the message of the book. There are five warnings in the Hebrews epistle which we will also consider. These are given to encourage us and not to frighten us, so please don't skip that chapter.

It isn't enough, however, to learn more about the book of Hebrews; we must also learn more about ourselves and take steps to improve our spiritual walk and the work of our churches. We must start with ourselves. We can't do it alone; we need each other. That's why the writer says, "Let *us*."

If you have never read the entire book of Hebrews, I recommend you do so before reading this book. Please keep your Bible at hand and look up and read the references cited. Remember, you are reading this book so that you might better understand God's Word.

"God . . . has spoken to us by his Son. . . . See to it that you do not refuse him who speaks" (Heb. 1:1–2; 12:25).

2

What Jesus Is Doing in Heaven for Us Today

If you were to ask ten Christians to explain what Jesus is now doing in heaven for His church on earth, two might give you a biblical answer, but the other eight would probably have very little to say. Their silence explains why they and many other Christians are stumbling and staggering instead of walking straight and marching strong: they are ignorant of the tremendous resources available from their Lord and Savior who is now exalted in heaven.

Jesus ascended to heaven forty days after His resurrection and was enthroned at the right hand of the Father. Ten days later, on the Day of Pentecost, the Holy Spirit came upon the church to equip and empower the saints for their walk, witness and work on earth until Jesus returns (see Acts 1–2). But we can't assume that most believers understand the ministry of the Lord Jesus Christ in heaven today. If they did, their Christian walk would be different. The Book of Hebrews was written to explain who Jesus is, where He is and what He is doing today.

That word "today" is important; the writer uses it eight times in the book (1:5; 3:7, 13, 15; 4:7 [twice]; 5:5 and 13:8). Many people think that Jesus is in heaven praying for the world so that lost sinners might be saved, *but that's the one thing He said He would not be doing!* He prayed for lost sinners as He hung on the cross—"Father, forgive them, for they do not know what they are doing" (Luke 23:34)—but in John 17:9, He said, "I am not praying for the world, but for those you have given me, for they are yours." If you are a Christian believer for whom nobody on earth is praying, you can be sure that the Son of God in heaven is interceding for you! "Therefore he is able to save completely [forever] those who come to God through him, because he always lives to intercede for them" (Heb. 7:25).

Hebrews is a book that can make conquerors out of quitters and winners out of potential losers.

The book of Hebrews begins like a theological essay, continues like a sermon and ends like a letter, but the writer calls it a "word of exhortation," or encouragement (13:22).

The repetition of "we" and "us" suggests that the writer is a preacher who is speaking to all of us. This "sermon" is a powerful encouragement to faithfulness, letting believers know that Jesus is with them and praying for them. It is also a loving warning to keep believers from turning back to the old life. His readers were suffering for their faith. They were in danger of giving up on the Christian life and turning back to Judaism. He wrote this epistle to urge them not to go back but to *go in, go on, go up* and *go out.* If only they would trust God, the same Word that saved them would also strengthen and sustain them. Hebrews is a book that can make conquerors out of quitters and winners out of potential losers.

This constant intercession of our Lord includes eight wonderful ministries, some of which may be new or foreign to you. Let's begin our study of Hebrews by discovering what these ministries are.

Jesus Is Speaking (Hebrews 1:1–2)

That God would speak at all to sinful people like us is certainly an act of grace, and that He would send His only Son, His beloved Son, to do the speaking is even more astounding. In the past God had spoken in various ways and at different times, but Jesus came as "God's last Word" (see John 1:1–5, 14). "Last of all, he sent his son to them" (Matt. 21:37). All the rivers of divine revelation converge upon Jesus, whose voice is "like the sound of rushing waters" (Rev. 1:15). This Word from God is *powerful* and brought the universe into being (see Heb. 1:3). Paul called it "the word of life" (Phil. 2:16) and "the word of his grace" (Acts 20:32) and "the word of Christ" that generates saving faith in our hearts (Rom. 10:17). What a Word!

The way we treat the written Word of God is the way we treat the living Word of God, Jesus Christ. We cannot ignore the Bible and at the same time honor Jesus Christ.

But don't put this Word in the past tense. We don't hear an audible voice as prophets did in the Old Testament and apostles in the New Testament. But through the Scriptures God is still speaking to His people through His Son. The author of Hebrews admonishes us in the present tense, "See to it that you do not refuse him who speaks" (12:25). If our hearts are truly prepared, each time we open the Bible and pray, God will open His mouth and speak to our minds and hearts (see 1 Sam. 3:10). *The way we treat the written Word of God is the way we treat the living Word of God, Jesus Christ.* We cannot ignore the Bible and at the same time honor Jesus Christ.

It's important to note that the emphasis in Hebrews is on *speaking* and *hearing* and not on *seeing*. The nation of Israel heard God speak at Sinai but did not see any form of God, and they were warned not to make idols or images (see Exod. 20:4;

Deut. 4:12–15). We're living in a day that emphasizes the visual and minimizes the spoken word. But the Spirit of God can speak to our hearts as we read and study the Word and as His servants expound it to us at worship. The Spirit doesn't need our clever gimmicks to get the point across.

Jesus Is Sustaining (Hebrews 1:3)

Jesus not only created all things through His Word, but He constantly sustains everything He has created. The Greek word translated "sustaining" conveys three wonderful truths: (1) Jesus is holding everything up so it won't fall, (2) He is holding everything together so it won't fall apart and (3) He is carrying creation along to a predetermined goal. Scientists know about atoms and subatomic particles, *but they cannot explain what holds it all together*. "He [Jesus] is before all things, and in him all things hold together" (Col. 1:17).

Now, if Jesus Christ is able to hold up the universe and hold it together, can't He also keep our lives and ministries from falling down or falling apart? Can't He carry us along to fulfill the divine purposes for which He saved us? "For we are God's workmanship, created in Christ Jesus to do good works, which God prepared in advance for us to do" (Eph. 2:10). What an encouragement! What a responsibility!

Jesus Is Sitting (Hebrews 1:3)

This doesn't sound like much of a ministry, for almost anybody can sit; but consider where He is sitting and why He is there. He is seated at the right hand of the Father in heaven, the place of honor, power and authority, *because He has finished His work!*

> Lifted up was He to die,
> "It is finished!" was His cry;
> Now in heaven exalted high:
> Hallelujah, what a Savior![1]

There were no chairs in the Jewish tabernacle because the priests' work was never completed. Why? Because the blood of animal sacrifices, offered day after day and year after year, could never wash away sins (see Heb. 10:1–14); but "the blood of Jesus, his Son, purifies us from all sin" (1 John 1:7). Jesus is seated today on a glorious throne of sovereign power and authority. He has defeated every enemy. There is nothing more that He must do to save lost sinners, encourage struggling believers or enable dedicated pilgrims to continue their faith journey. If we trust Him, He will carry us through. Jesus isn't nervously pacing the streets of gold, worrying about the future of His people. He is calmly sitting on the throne, and He has everything under control.

Jesus Is Bringing (Hebrews 2:10)

He is "bringing many sons and daughters to glory." Jesus doesn't just save sinners by dying for them; He lives *for* His people and *in* them by His Spirit and sees to it that they ultimately arrive at the Father's house (see John 14:1–6). One day He will say, "Here am I, and the children God has given me" (Heb. 2:13; see also Isa. 8:18), and not one of them will be lost. "Therefore he is able to save completely [forever] those who come to God through him, because he always lives to intercede for them" (Heb. 7:25). Jesus is the "author and perfecter of our faith" (12:2), and the work He begins, He will complete. Today and every day, Jesus intercedes for us so that He may one day have the joy of presenting us to the Father (see Jude 24).

Jesus Is Sympathizing (Hebrews 4:14–16)

Aaron and his descendants were high priests, but Jesus is our "great high priest who has gone through the heavens" (Heb. 4:14). As a part of his official dress, Aaron wore a jewel on each shoulder with the names of six of the twelve tribes engraved on each one. He also wore twelve jewels on the breastplate, one for each tribe. He bore his people on his shoulders and over his heart. *Jesus does that for us in heaven today in a far greater way.*

The word *sympathize* usually brings to our minds the picture of an adult consoling a child and kissing away the tears. Jesus doesn't "feel sorry for us" and pamper us. Instead, He feels *with us* and gives us the strength we need to bear the burden, even if we don't always understand what's happening. During His ministry on earth, He experienced the tests and temptations we face; He can "sympathize with our weaknesses" (4:15) and is able to help us. Jesus doesn't sympathize with our sins, but He does sympathize with our struggle, for He understands the human weaknesses that can lead us to sin. When we come to the throne of grace in prayer, we can always "receive mercy and find grace to help us in our time of need" (4:16). Faith lives on promises, not on explanations. When we are tempted to say with David that "no one is concerned for me" or "no one cares for my life" (Ps. 142:4), we must remember that Jesus cares for His own and will never forsake them (94:14). His sympathy is far more than loving feelings; it's divine action that helps us keep going for His glory.

We can always "receive mercy and find grace to help us in our time of need."

David asked, "What is man that you are mindful of him, the son of man that you care for him?" (Ps. 8:4). The answer is that we are made in God's image, loved by God, purchased by God's Son and indwelt by God's Spirit. Therefore, "Cast all your anxiety on him because he cares for you" (1 Pet. 5:7). Did you read that? *He cares for you*!

Jesus Is Waiting Expectantly (Hebrews 10:11–14)

The word translated "waits" in verse 13 means "to be ready

and prepared for any situation." Our Lord is waiting but not resting or napping, for "he who watches over you will not slumber" (Ps. 121:3). Jesus knows what is going on and is never surprised by any situation; therefore, He is able to solve any problem, face any enemy or meet any need. When Jesus returned to heaven after His victory at Calvary, the Father said to Him, "Sit at my right hand until I make your enemies a footstool for your feet" (Ps. 110:1). This means that *the enemy is already defeated*!

From the book of Job to Revelation, God's people have cried out, "How long, O Lord, how long?" The prophet Habakkuk opened his book with, "How long, O LORD, must I call for help, but you do not listen?" (1:2), and even the martyrs in heaven ask, "How long, Sovereign Lord, holy and true, until you judge the inhabitants of the earth and avenge our blood?" (Rev. 6:10). "When is the Lord going to do something?" is a question God's people often ask, and the answer is, "When the time is right." Jesus is on the throne and He knows what time it is, so there's no need for us to fret. It is "through faith and patience" that we inherit the promises of God.

Jesus Is Preparing (Hebrews 11:16)

Until Jesus began His public ministry, He worked as a carpenter, making and repairing plows, furniture, buildings and other necessary items. Today in heaven He is still building. "I am going there to prepare a place for you," He told His disciples (John 14:2). Hebrews 11:16 tells us that a heavenly city is being prepared for all who trust Him, who, as "aliens and strangers" in this world, look forward to moving out of their tents and into God's glorious city (see Heb. 11:13–16). Heaven is a prepared place for a prepared people. Just as parents prepare a place for an expected child, and just as a bridegroom prepares a place for his beloved wife-to-be, so Jesus is preparing a place for His family and His Bride in glory. David was right: "Surely goodness and love will follow me all the days of my life, and I will dwell in the house of the LORD forever" (Ps. 23:6).

Jesus Is Equipping (Hebrews 13:20–21)

From His throne in heaven, Jesus by His Spirit is equipping His people for life and service now and also preparing us for further service when we enter His glorious kingdom, just as the master prepared the servants to invest their talents wisely while he was away (see Matt. 25:14–30). The verb "equip" in Hebrews 13:21 is the Greek word *katartizo*, which means "to furnish, to complete." In the ancient Greek world, this word meant "to rig a ship" to be ready for the voyage or "to equip an army" for the battle. It is used in Matthew 4:21 for mending nets and preparing to go out for a catch. Doctors used the word for setting a broken bone to prepare a patient to return to normal life. Note that *katartizo* also has our English word "artist" in it. If we submit to Him day by day, Jesus, the Master Artist, will work in us, equipping us to serve Him the way He wants us to serve. We should get all the education, training and experience we can, but without God's equipping our service will be useless. "Apart from me," said Jesus, "you can do nothing" (John 15:5).

It was a joyful day in my life when I discovered how the Lord had "wired me" and what He wanted me to do with my life. Everything fell into place, and I've tried to keep that vision in clear focus ever since. Years ago, Dr. Torrey Johnson, one of the founders of Youth for Christ, told me, "Find the one thing you do that God blesses, *and stay with it*!" I recommend his words to you.

These eight ministries are but the tip of the iceberg. As you read Hebrews and meditate on what you read, the Spirit will show you more and more of Christ's sufficiency for your every need. The Lord never commands without enabling, and that enablement comes from the Savior's throne of grace in heaven. When we study Hebrews 7–10, we'll learn more about the spiritual resources we have in heaven and what it means to worship in Spirit and truth.

Finally, keep in mind that our Lord's intercessory ministry is possible because of His life on earth, His death on the cross and

His resurrection from the dead. When Jesus returned to heaven, He had a glorified body, *but that body still bears the wounds from the cross!* Not "scars," please note, but "wounds" (see John 20:20, 24–29). The blessings He shares with us day by day were purchased by His shed blood on the cross, and we must never take them lightly.

The Message of Hebrews Is for Us Today

We don't know who wrote the book of Hebrews or to whom it was originally sent, but we do know why it was written and why those unknown saints needed to read it and take its instruction to heart.

The recipients of the letter were Jewish believers who had come to faith in Christ through the witness of people who had been eyewitnesses of Christ's ministry (see Heb. 2:1–4). I'm a Gentile, but my spiritual situation is similar to theirs because, by faith, I'm a child of Abraham (see Gal. 3:7–9) and, like Abraham, I'm an "alien and stranger" in his world (see Heb. 11:13–16; 1 Pet. 1:1; 2:11). The word "Hebrew" comes from the Hebrew word *eber*, which means "a stranger, a pilgrim, a person on the move" (see Gen. 10:24–25). Abraham was a foreigner in the land of Canaan and lived in tents, but, like believers today, he looked for the heavenly city prepared for all who have been saved by faith (see Heb. 11:13–16).

The next time you read the book of Revelation, note that the unsaved people are called "those who live on the earth" (Rev. 3:10; 11:10; 14:6) or "the inhabitants of the earth" (6:10; 8:13; 11:10; 13:12, 14). Why? Because true believers in Jesus Christ have their citizenship in heaven (see Phil. 3:20; Luke 10:20). We've been called out from this present evil age and belong to the family of God (see John 17:14–16; Gal. 1:3–5). That's why we set our attention and affection on "things above," where Jesus is enthroned, and not on earthly things (see Col. 3:1–2). In his book *Free in Obedience*, William Stringfellow wrote, "Contemporary Christians can be enlightened by turning to Hebrews both about the situations of their predecessors and their own situations. Or, to put it a bit differently, the Christians today *are* the Hebrews."[2]

The saints who received the Hebrew epistle had been saved long enough to be teachers of the Word, but instead of teaching, they were gradually going backward in their spiritual walk and had to learn their ABCs over again (Heb. 5:11–14). In the past they had suffered for their faith and had remained faithful, but now they were losing ground (10:32–34). They were forgetting their past teachers and the lessons they had taught (13:7–10) and were losing confidence in their present spiritual leaders (Heb. 13:17). Their spiritual temperature was so low that some of them had quit attending the fellowship and were on the verge of going back into Judaism with all its traditions (4:14; 10:19–25; 13:9–10). They forgot their heavenly citizenship, and they forgot they were strangers on this earth.

The book of Hebrews was written to help bring "spiritual recovery" to this group of believers who wanted to be safe and comfortable in a society that opposed the Christian faith. The Roman government tolerated the Jewish faith, so if these believers returned to Judaism, they would be protected from persecution. But instead of going back to the old life, they should have gone "outside the camp" and suffered disgrace for Jesus (13:11–14), and moved forward in their new lives in Christ (6:1–3). If they went back into the security of the synagogue and the temple, it meant ignoring the letter to the Galatians and the decision in Acts 15 and trying to mix Judaism and Christianity.

The Christian life is so constituted that, if we stand still, we will fall back, so the only solution is to grow in grace and move forward. "Therefore let us leave the elementary teachings about Christ and go on to maturity" (Heb. 6:1). (I will have more to say about this when we study chapters 5–6 and 11–13.) Let us beware of the forces at work in the church today that encourage compromise rather than separation from and confrontation with today's antichristian world. In *Dining with the Devil*, Os

Guinness writes, "Far from leading an exodus, modern church growth often uses the ideology and tools of Egypt to make the life of the people of God more comfortable in captivity."[3] That's what these discouraged Jewish believers wanted: comfort in captivity. And where would they find it? Back in the synagogue and the temple.

How did the writer deal with this problem and seek to solve it?

First, he exalted Jesus Christ and showed that He was greater than the angels, Moses and Joshua, and that the "spiritual rest" He gives is far greater than anything Judaism has to offer (Heb. 1–4). Then the writer affirmed the dependability of God's promises (Heb. 5–6) and the sufficiency of God's heavenly provisions for their lives (Heb. 7–10). These things being true, he urged them not to look for personal security but to grow in spiritual maturity and courageous ministry outside the camp. Rather than going backward, they should be going forward, moving out into the needy world, sharing the message of Christ and demonstrating its significance in their lives.

If you haven't yet read the book of Hebrews, I suggest you pause now and do so. If you have read it, then take time to read and review chapters 1–4. If your Old Testament history is rusty, read the passages that are referenced in this chapter or in your Bible cross references. Please note in Hebrews 1–4 that the emphasis is on Jesus Christ. It's a call to give Jesus the preeminence in our lives and to depend wholly on His grace.

Jesus in Hebrews 1, truly God:

- God's Son (1:2, 5, 8)
- Heir of all things (1:2)
- Creator (1:2, 10)
- Radiance of God's glory (1:3)
- Representation of God's being (1:3)
- Sustainer of all things (1:3)

- Savior (1:3)
- King (1:3)
- Firstborn (1:6)
- Victor (1:13)
- Greater than the angels (1:4–14)

Jesus in Hebrews 2, truly Man:

- The last Adam (2:5–8)
- The glorified Sacrifice (2:9)
- The resurrected Brother (2:10–13)
- The Redeemer from death and Satan (2:14–16)
- The sympathetic High Priest (2:17–18)

3

Victory—Let's Go In!

Claiming Our Spiritual Inheritance
Hebrews 1–4

But he brought us out from there [Egypt] to bring us in and give us the land that he promised on oath to our forefathers.
Deuteronomy 6:23

The first four chapters of Hebrews focus on three important geographic locations in the history of Israel: the land of Egypt, the wilderness and the promised land of Canaan. Except for a burial cave that Abraham purchased (see Gen. 23; 49:29–32), the patriarchs never possessed any property in Canaan. They were foreigners and strangers in the land, just as God's people are in this world today. It was not until Joshua and the army of Israel entered Canaan and conquered it (see Josh. 1–12) that the people of Israel possessed their promised inheritance.

Geography and Theology

Old Testament history and geography help us to understand New Testament theology. Israel in Egypt pictures the sinner's bondage to the world and the flesh, while Israel delivered from Egypt depicts salvation by the blood of the Lamb and the power of God (Exod. 12–15). Israel in the wilderness illustrates the sad consequences God's people experience when they refuse to trust God and rebel against Him in unbelief (Num. 13–14). Israel dwelling in Canaan illustrates the victorious life of faith that claims the inheritance God has for each of us in Jesus Christ. We are "blessed . . . with every spiritual blessing in Christ" (Eph. 1:3).

It's unfortunate that some poets and composers have misinterpreted these Old Testament events and completely missed their message. Crossing the Jordan River is not a picture of death ("I don't want to cross Jordan alone"), and entering Canaan is not a picture of going to heaven ("Land me safe on Canaan's shore"). Surely we won't fight wars in heaven as Israel did in Canaan! When Israel crossed the Red Sea, they said good-bye to the bondage of Egypt. When they disobeyed God and refused to enter Canaan, they wandered in the wilderness and missed the "rest" God had promised them. After four decades in the wilderness, they finally crossed the Jordan River by faith and entered Canaan and claimed their inheritance.

During the forty years between the Exodus from Egypt and the entrance into Canaan, Israel frequently complained about their circumstances and wanted to go back to Egypt. The people who received the epistle to the Hebrews had the same problem: they were being persecuted and were considering forsaking their rich inheritance in Christ and going back to the old life in Judaism. Even today, many Christians are "betweeners," living between Egypt and Canaan and unwilling to exercise faith, claim their victory in Christ and enter their inheritance.

Along with the Lord Himself, the heroes of Israel's Egypt-to-Canaan story are the angels, Moses the prophet, Aaron the high priest and Joshua, Moses' successor and the general of the Jewish army. The angels watched over Israel at the Exodus and during their wilderness trek and also assisted in the giving of the Law at Sinai (Exod. 14:19; 23:20, 23; Gal. 3:19). Aaron died at Mount Hor, near the border of Edom (Num. 20:22–29). Moses led the Jews out of Egypt to the border of Canaan where he died (Deut. 34), and Joshua brought Israel into Canaan.

As we study Hebrews 1–4, we discover two important truths. First, we learn that Jesus is greater than the angels (1:4–2:18), Moses (3:1–4:13), Aaron (4:14–5:14) and Joshua (4:1–13). Second, we learn that Moses, Aaron and Joshua were unable to give a complete inheritance to Israel. Though they did what God told them to do, in one way or another they all fell short. Aaron never made it even to the border of Canaan. Moses got to the border but wasn't permitted to lead the people into the land (Num. 20:1–13; Deut. 34). Joshua took Israel into the land but was unable to give them the rest God promised them (Heb. 4:8–11).

Jesus is superior to the greatest of men and all the angels, and deserves our highest adoration and obedience. He is all we need.

Moses as the prophet represents God's law, but "the law made nothing perfect" and was only a "shadow" of the good things Jesus would provide (Heb. 7:19; 10:1). Aaron, as a high priest, represents the Jewish sacrificial system, which could "never, by the same sacrifices repeated endlessly year after year, make perfect those who draw near to worship." Why? Because "it is impossible for the blood of bulls and goats to take away sins" (10:1, 4). Joshua, as the general, represents a king and led the people into Canaan. Moses, Aaron and Joshua—the human representatives of the offices of prophet, priest (see 7:11) and king—could make nothing perfect. Only Jesus Christ can do that.

The conclusion is obvious: for the recipients of this letter to abandon Jesus and return to Judaism would mean forsaking God's perfect Savior and turning to "redeemers" who could not redeem. Why go back to that which is imperfect and abandon the perfect Son of God (see 2:10; 5:9)? Jesus is superior to the greatest of men and all the angels, and deserves our highest adoration and obedience. *He is all we need* (see 2:10).

Our Double Inheritance

Canaan was Israel's inheritance, given by God to His people. Joshua led Israel into Canaan, conquered the land and assigned to each tribe the inheritance God marked out for them (see Josh. 13–22). Christian believers are God's "firstborn" (Heb. 12:23) and have a double inheritance from our heavenly Father (see Deut. 21:15–17). Most people think of a heavenly inheritance—mansions in heaven—when they think of an inheritance from God. When Jesus comes again, we will receive our future inheritance in His glorious kingdom (see Rom. 8:17; Eph. 5:5; Col. 3:24; Heb. 9:15; 1 Pet. 1:4). But *today*—right now—we have a rich spiritual inheritance in Christ that marks out our sphere of ministry and provides all that we need to fulfill our calling (see Acts 20:32; Col. 1:12). In Second Corinthians 10:13–17, Paul discusses this present inheritance. Read his words carefully.

> We, however, will not boast beyond proper limits, but will confine our boasting to the field God has assigned to us, a field that reaches even to you. We are not going too far in our boasting, as would be the case if we had not come to you, for we did get as far as you with the gospel of Christ. Neither do we go beyond our limits by boasting of work done by others. Our hope is that, as your faith continues to grow, our area of activity among you will greatly expand, so that we can preach the gospel in the regions beyond you. For we do not want to boast about work already done in another man's territory. But, "Let him who boasts boast in the Lord."

Before God saved Saul of Tarsus, He had already determined that Saul would become Paul, the apostle to the Gentiles (see Acts 9:15; 22:21; Gal. 1:13–16; 2:1–2, 7–10; Eph. 3:1–12; 1 Tim. 2:7). God had marked out the "sphere of his ministry," and Paul was careful to obey. "It has always been my ambition to preach the gospel where Christ was not known, so that I would not be building on someone else's foundation" (Rom. 15:20). That was Paul's inheritance, and it included God's guarantee that

Paul's every need would be met. King David had a similar view of his life and ministry.

> Lord, you have assigned my portion and my cup;
> you have made my lot secure.
> The boundary lines have fallen for me in pleasant places;
> surely I have a delightful inheritance. (Ps. 16:5–6)

It's all so beautifully summarized by Paul in Ephesians 2:10: "For we are God's workmanship, created in Christ Jesus to do good works, which God prepared in advance for us to do." God's people must do God's will for God's glory where He wants it done and how He wants it done. If we obey, we will always have God's direction, provision and protection. "For it is God who works in you to will and to act according to his good purpose" (Phil. 2:13). God works in us and through us so that He might be glorified in us. As we abide in Christ, His life at work in us enables us to bear fruit (John 15:1–5).

The Promised Rest

There is one more matter concerning our inheritance that must be addressed, and that's the rest that God promised His ancient people and also promises Christian believers today. Eleven times in Hebrews 1–4 you find the word "rest" as a noun or a verb (3:11, 18; 4:1, 3, 4, 5, 8, 9, 10, 11), and these references speak of four different rests:

1. God's Sabbath rest when He completed creation (4:4, 10; see Gen. 2:1–3)
2. Israel's rest from war after conquering Canaan (3:11, 18; 4:4–5, 8; Deut. 12:8–10; 25:19; Josh. 1:13–15; 21:43–45; Ps. 95)
3. The rest we have when we trust Christ and yield our all to Him (4:1–3, 10–11; Matt. 11:28–30; Rom. 5:1; Phil. 4:4–7)
4. The future eternal rest of believers in heaven (4:9; Rev. 14:13)

Rest number 3 is the heart rest God's children experience when we yield ourselves entirely to the Lord and daily take His yoke and learn from Him. It's the "peace of God" that is neither isolation from trials and difficulties nor insulation from pain and pressures, but calmness and control *in the midst of the difficulties around us and the enemies against us*. It's simply being like Jesus when everything seems to be falling apart (see Luke 8:22–25).

When Jesus was slandered and criticized, He calmly spoke the truth or else remained silent. When a storm raged over the Sea of Galilee, He lay in the boat sleeping and then awakened to calm the storm. When the officers arrived in the garden to arrest Him, He stepped forward and surrendered, and protected His frightened disciples. When He was illegally tried and falsely accused by wicked men, He said nothing. While being nailed to the cross, He prayed for those who sinned against Him. Without complaint, He suffered six hours of horrible pain. "When they hurled their insults at him, he did not retaliate; when he suffered, he made no threats. Instead, he entrusted himself to him who judges justly" (1 Pet. 2:23). That is "the peace of God, which transcends all understanding" (Phil. 4:7). It's part of our wonderful inheritance in Christ that we can claim by faith.

During Israel's years of wandering in the wilderness, there were two men in the camp, Joshua and Caleb, who never complained but instead looked forward to enjoying the Promised Land, their place of rest on this earth. Two years after fleeing Egypt the Israelites spied out the land of Canaan. Joshua and Caleb were the only two spies who did not die when God struck the other ten spies for their unbelief (see Num. 14; Deut. 1:34–36). Everybody in the camp who, at the time, was twenty years old or older died in the wilderness during the next thirty-eight years, but Joshua and Caleb were the only two who had the joyful privilege of bringing a new generation into their inheritance. It is sad to think that the unfaithful spies not only missed their inheritance—their rest—but influenced thousands of others to miss theirs as well.

How many people did Joshua and Caleb help to bury as the old generation died off? How many grieving relatives did they comfort? How did they keep from grumbling along with their neighbors when God disciplined the nation and they had to suffer with them? They believed the Word of God and obeyed the will of God and therefore experienced the peace of God in their hearts. Caleb and Joshua were in the wilderness physically, but they were in their inheritance spiritually, and were drawing upon God's help for each daily task.

We are not only saved by faith, but we also must live by faith so that we can claim our full inheritance and find our rest in Jesus, who wants to give us life to the full.

At some point after Israel's experience at Kadesh-Barnea (see Num. 13–14), God inspired a priest or Levite to write about that tragic rebellion. We know it as Psalm 95, and I suggest that you pause now and carefully read that psalm.

Most of the psalms end on a positive note, but you will notice that this psalm ends with an angry verdict: "They shall never enter my rest" (95:11). That statement is quoted three times in Hebrews (3:11; 4:3, 5), and Scripture explains why this judgment was so severe: the nation of Israel hardened their hearts and refused to believe that God would do what He promised (see Ps. 95:8; Heb. 3:8, 15; 4:7). And what caused their hearts to harden? The writer calls it "sin's deceitfulness" (Heb. 3:13).

If we follow the bad example of Israel and walk by sight, rejecting God's Word, we can never see temptation and sin in their true character. Temptation seems like a splendid opportunity to obtain something or enjoy something and not have to pay for it, or to have pleasure that will never turn into pain. Like Eve, we believe Satan's lies: "Did God really say, 'You must not . . . ? . . .

You will not surely die. . . . You will be like God'" (Gen. 3:1–4). Satan was saying, "Go ahead and eat! There are no absolutes, there are no consequences, and you will be a better person for doing it." This is the essence of the deceitfulness of sin! If we don't trust God, we tempt God, and there are serious consequences to tempting God, such as the hardening of the heart.

We must beware of "a sinful, unbelieving heart that turns away from the living God" (Heb. 3:12), i.e., a heart that defies or ignores His Word. While a covetous heart and a sensual heart are sinful, God says that *an unbelieving heart* is wicked and the seedbed for many sins and restlessness. Unbelief is so dangerous because it makes God a liar and robs us of the spiritual power we need to overcome the Enemy. Hebrews, Romans and Galatians are the three New Testament books that explain the Old Testament belief that "the righteous will live by his faith" (Hab. 2:4, NASB; Rom. 1:17; Gal. 3:11; Heb. 10:38). We are not only saved by faith (Eph. 2:8–9), but we also must live by faith so that we can claim our full inheritance and find our rest in Jesus, who wants to give us life to the full (see John 10:10).

Enter the Holy Spirit

After listing some of the gracious acts that the Lord performed for Israel, Isaiah adds, "Yet they rebelled and grieved his Holy Spirit" (63:10), and Asaph wrote in Psalm 78:40, "How often they rebelled against him in the desert and grieved him in the wasteland!" In Acts 7:51, as Stephen concluded his defense before the elders of Israel, he spoke these cutting words: "You stiff-necked people, with uncircumcised hearts and ears! You are just like your fathers: You always resist the Holy Spirit!" The people responded not by repenting but by stoning him to death. The sins of the fathers show up in the children.

We can point to ourselves as well. Paul warned the early Christians, "do not grieve the Holy Spirit of God, with whom you were sealed for the day of redemption" (Eph. 4:30). The Israelites who died in the wilderness never saw their "day of redemption" because they were guilty of grieving the Spirit of God, a sin we commit today. That is why Paul commands us to be filled with the Holy Spirit of God, and in Ephesians 5:17–21 he gives us three marks of Spirit-controlled believers: joyfulness (5:19), thankfulness (5:20) and submissiveness (5:21). Read the passage and mark it.

Like the book of Hebrews, Psalm 95 contains "let us" statements. There are five of them:

> "Let us sing for joy to the Lord" (95:1)
> "Let us shout aloud to the Rock of our salvation" (95:1)
> "Let us come before him with thanksgiving" (95:2)
> "Let us bow down in worship" (95:6)
> "Let us kneel before the Lord our Maker" (95:6)

The first two statements say, "Let's be joyful!" The third one says, "Let's be thankful!" The last two say, "Let's submit to the Lord and to each other, like sheep." Joy, gratitude and submission are the very marks of Spirit-controlled believers, according to Ephesians 5:17–21!

Now we can better understand how Israel grieved the Spirit and missed claiming their inheritance: because they didn't receive God's Word and allow it to work in their hearts. "Today, if you hear his voice . . ." (Ps. 95:7; see also Heb. 3:7, 15; 4:7). Now, let's consider the marks of believers who are filled with the Word of God, as found in Colossians 3:16–4:1.

> Let the word of Christ dwell in you richly as you teach and admonish one another with all wisdom, and as you sing psalms, hymns and spiritual songs with gratitude in your hearts to God. And whatever you do, whether in word or deed, do it all in the name of the Lord Jesus, giving thanks to God the Father through him. Wives, submit to your husbands. . . . Husbands, love your wives. . . . Children, obey your parents. . . . Slaves, obey your earthly masters. . . . Masters, provide your slaves with what is right and fair.

If we are filled with the Word of God, we will be joyful, thankful and submissive; but to be filled with the Spirit of God also means to be joyful, thankful and submissive. In other words, the way we treat the Scriptures is the way we treat the Spirit of God, the author of the Scriptures. If, like Israel, we ignore or deliberately disobey God's Word, we will grieve God's Spirit and not be able to enter our inheritance and claim the blessing.

Claiming the Inheritance Today

When we trusted Jesus Christ as our Lord and Savior, we immediately received the title deed to our *eternal* inheritance (Heb. 9:15), but we must claim our *present* inheritance by faith. Just as Joshua led Israel into the Promised Land, so Jesus leads His people today into the inheritance marked out for them. Joshua is a type of Jesus; both names mean "Jehovah is salvation." Joshua 3–4 describes how Israel entered the land and gives the example for us to follow.

If, like Israel, we ignore or deliberately disobey God's Word, we will grieve God's Spirit and not be able to enter our inheritance and claim the blessing.

We must believe God (Josh. 3:1–13). God gave Joshua the commandment to prepare the people for crossing the Jordan, and Joshua passed it along to the officers and the people. Unlike the ten disbelieving spies thirty-eight years before, the officers and people united in hearing and believing God's Word. They consecrated themselves to the Lord and were able to do the impossible because they knew God was with them. "So faith comes from hearing, and hearing by the word of Christ" (Rom. 10:17, NASB). God promised to open the waters before them as He did at the Red Sea and to give Israel total victory over their enemies. Review the section "Our Double Inheritance" (page 28), and let

God make His promises real to your own heart.

We must obey God (Josh. 3:14–17). Their father Abraham had to step out by faith in order to claim the inheritance God gave him (Gen. 13:14–18), and Joshua and Israel had to do the same thing. The ark that preceded them represented the throne of God, and during the crossing, the Lord kept the waters back until all Israel had entered the land. Faith means obeying God in spite of the feelings within us, the circumstances around us or the consequences before us.

We must glorify God (Josh. 4:1–24). The Israelites built the stone monument on the bank of the river not to magnify the name of Israel or Joshua but to glorify the name of the Lord. It marked the place where God had brought His people safely into the Promised Land. In years to come, when new generations asked about the meaning of the stones on the bank of the Jordan River, the answer pointed to the Lord and glorified Him just as the crossing of the Jordan brought glory to God among "all the peoples of the earth" (4:23–24). The enemies Israel faced in Canaan heard about the parting of the Jordan and were terrified (5:1), and this prepared them to fear the Jewish army.

These, then, are the essentials for claiming our inheritance today: we must believe God, obey God and glorify God. We must give ourselves wholly to the Lord and pray, "Hallowed be your name . . . your will be done" (Matt. 6:9–10). But these steps must be taken today and every day. "Today, if you hear his voice, do not harden your hearts" (Ps. 95:7–8; see also Heb. 3:7–8, 15; 4:7). Each time we resist God, we harden our hearts more, and this grieves the Spirit of God. Every day, Joshua and his people had to present themselves to God and take the steps outlined above. Whenever Joshua ran ahead of the Lord and didn't seek His guidance, he failed miserably. Had he prayed before attacking Ai, he would have discovered the traitor Achan in the camp and avoided temporary defeat (Josh. 7). Had he paused to seek God's will when the Gibeonites asked for a treaty, he would not have formed an alliance with his enemies (Josh. 9).

We must spend time daily in the Word of God and go to the throne of grace in prayer, or we will drift away from the Lord (Heb. 2:1–4). Neglecting the Word and prayer ultimately leads to deliberately turning away from God in unbelief and living in defeat (3:12–19). Read Exodus 17:8–16 for a description of Joshua's first battle after Israel left Egypt, and note that Moses, Aaron and Hur interceded on the mountain while Joshua and his army wielded their swords against the enemy in the valley. It takes both prayer and the sword to achieve the victory. The word "sword" is used seventeen times in the book of Joshua where the conquest of Canaan is recorded. When Joshua saw Jesus, He was carrying a sword (Josh. 5:13–15). The Christian's sword is the Word of God, and we must use it on ourselves as well as against the Enemy (Heb. 4:12–13). Just as Joshua defeated his enemies with prayer and the sword, we also must daily turn to the Word of God and go to the throne of grace and pray because that is how we claim our inheritance and have victory (see Heb. 4:14–16; Acts 6:4; Eph. 6:17–18).

Let's go in and claim our inheritance! "This is the victory that has overcome the world, even our faith" (1 John 5:4).

4

Maturity—Let's Go On!

Growing Up in the Christian Life
Hebrews 4:14–6:20

Therefore let us leave the elementary teachings about Christ and go on to maturity.
Hebrews 6:1

Salvation is a launching pad and not a parking lot. When we experience new birth through faith in Jesus Christ, we enter God's family (see John 3:1–8) as infants who are expected to grow up. The very life of God dwells in us, and where there's life, there should be growth. That's why the author of this epistle wrote "let us . . . go on to maturity" (Heb. 6:1). Another translation is "let us be carried along." We don't manufacture maturity by our own efforts. Rather, we cooperate with the Lord and allow Him to "carry us along" from infancy to maturity. None of us has "arrived" yet; we're all still maturing and will be until Jesus returns (see Phil. 3:12–14).

Maturing people are people who *know* themselves, *accept* themselves, *develop* themselves and willingly *give* themselves to serve others. They don't pretend to be something they are not, nor do they try to impress people by attempting things they're not equipped or called by God to do (see Ps. 133). Maturing people develop the gifts and abilities God has given them. They give themselves to the Lord so He can use them to serve others and bring glory to His name. Maturing people are learning not to compete with others, but to compete with themselves.

Infants are handicapped. They can't care for themselves but depend on others to feed them, wash them, dress them and protect them. They can't walk or run and, although they can make noise and cry, they can't speak words. Infants have very little discernment and are liable to chew on anything. They can't defend themselves, and from a legal point of view, they can't inherit anything. To remain an infant (if we had the choice) would mean missing almost everything wonderful that human life has to offer. Yes, infants enjoy attention, protection and leisure, but they miss everything else.

God wants to "carry us along" by His power so that we will grow up and not just grow old.

God wants to "carry us along" by His power so that we will grow up and not just grow old. He wants us to "become mature, attaining to the whole measure of the fullness of Christ" (Eph. 4:13). Our own personal task and the task of church leaders is to "present everyone perfect in Christ" (Col. 1:28; see 4:12). Our faith in the Lord should grow (see 2 Thess.1:3) and so should our love for others (see 1 Thess. 3:12). We must "grow in the grace and knowledge of our Lord and Savior Jesus Christ" (2 Pet. 3:18). "Let's go on" involves growing.

A local church is a spiritual family made up of children, fathers and young people in the faith (see 1 John 2:12–14). All of them should be in the process of growing up and becoming more and more like the Lord Jesus Christ (see Eph. 4:15; 2 Cor. 3:18). The public ministry of the church must not be a dull routine with no spiritual nourishment for the family. New believers must be taught how to "feed themselves," so that daily they can enjoy the Word of God and prayer and experience growth. *Unless we have an appetite for God's Word, we will never mature as we should; and feeding on the wrong things will destroy our appetite for God.* A worship service or a Bible study should be an opportunity for spiritual enrichment and not just social enjoyment.

Three words summarize the message of the "Let's Go On" section of Hebrews: *ability*—God is able to carry us along (4:14–6:3); *impossibility*—we cannot lose our salvation (6:4–12); *dependability*—the Lord will see us through (6:13–20). If we come to the throne of grace and put our faith in the God of all grace, we will not easily fall into disgrace and bring shame upon ourselves and our Lord.

Ability—The Throne of Grace (Hebrews 4:14–6:3)

"Our God is able" is a major article of faith for all Christian believers. He "is able to help those who are being tempted" (Heb. 2:18). He is able to empathize with our weaknesses (4:15) and "is able to save completely [forever] those who come to God through him, because he always lives to intercede for them" (7:25). Jesus isn't a high priest like Aaron; He is the Great High Priest who belongs to "the order of Melchizedek" (5:5, 10), an important subject we will take up in the next chapter.

The heavenly throne of Jesus Christ is not a throne of judgment but a throne of grace, and the way to the throne was opened by Jesus when He died for us on the cross (see Heb. 10:19–23). We can approach His throne at any time with confidence ("freedom of speech") for He knows us intimately, He loves us and He will listen to us and give us the help we need. What do we obtain at His throne? We shall "receive mercy and find grace to help us in our time of need" (4:16). God, in His mercy, doesn't give us what we deserve: judgment; instead, He gives us what we don't deserve: grace. No matter what difficulties we may encounter, Jesus has already overcome. He experienced every trial and temptation and knows how to handle them; He gives us victory.

With a sympathetic and powerful high priest like Jesus, why should any of us fail? For the same reason the recipients of this epistle failed: they were not diligent; they were "lazy" in the disciplines of the Christian life (see Heb. 6:11–12). Just as our physical bodies require food, shelter and exercise in order to survive and grow, our spirit requires food (the Word), shelter (prayer) and exercise (resisting temptation and witnessing to others) in order to grow spiritually. It takes the encouragement of Christian family and friends and a deep desire to become more like Jesus. There's nothing automatic about becoming more like Jesus.

If we put as much personal discipline into our Christian life as we do our golf, tennis, swimming and other physical exercises—all of which are good—we would all be better Christians.

According to Hebrews 5:11–14, the people who first read this letter were slow to learn (5:11) and unable to share God's truth with others. They lived on the "milk of the Word" and not "solid food" (5:12–14). The "milk" is the truth about what Jesus did on earth—His birth, life, death and resurrection—truths that a child can learn. But the "solid food" has to do with what Jesus is now doing in heaven as a king and a priest like Melchizedek. Hebrews 7–10, which I cover in the next chapter, focuses on this theme and explains the practical meaning of Christ's ministry today.

The recipients of this letter not only lacked a good diet, but they neglected "exercise" and failed to put the Word of God into practice in their daily lives. The word translated "to train" in verse 14 gives us our English word "gymnasium." If we put as much personal discipline into our Christian life as we do our golf, tennis, swimming and other physical exercises—all of which are good—we would all be better Christians. I've known Christians who could recite sports statistics without an error, but they couldn't find Jonah or Romans in their Bibles. They wouldn't dare miss their Sunday games, but they rarely read the Word of God, and their church attendance is erratic.

These "lazy" believers also lacked discernment. Just as young children need constant supervision lest they get into things they shouldn't, eat the wrong foods or choose the wrong friends, so immature Christians are easily tempted by the world (see James 1:27) and the flesh (see Gal. 5:19–21). Paul prayed that the saints in Philippi might cultivate discernment so that they might choose the very best (see Phil. 1:9–11), and we need to pray that prayer for ourselves.

Jesus Christ is able. His throne of grace is accessible. Let's stop making excuses and go on to maturity!

Impossibility—The Sin of Disgrace (Hebrews 6:4–12)

This section of Hebrews has been a stumbling block to some Bible students, especially new believers, because it seems to teach that we can lose our salvation. But if you connect the first three words of verse 4 with six words in verse 6, it says, "It is impossible . . . [for them] to be brought back to repentance." *If this section describes believers who "lose their salvation," then it also affirms that these people cannot be restored!* I know people who believe Christians can "lose their salvation" more than once and still be forgiven and restored each time. But these verses say that if you can lose your salvation, it's impossible to be restored. Let's agree, then, that once people have been born again, they cannot be unborn.

Some students say, "But the people described in Hebrews 6:1–6 aren't really saved. They are on the road to salvation but haven't yet arrived." However, if they will connect these verses with Hebrews 6:9–12 and 10:32–35, they will discover that the writer of the letter considered his readers to be saved people. They had been faithful Christians in the past and even suffered for their faith, and now they were tempted to go back to the old foundation of Judaism. The doctrines named in Hebrews 6:1–2 are basic to the Jewish faith and compatible with the Christian faith, but there's a difference in foundations. The foundation for the Christian faith is our Lord Jesus Christ. That foundation was laid by the ministry of the apostles (see 1 Cor. 3:10–12; Eph. 2:20). The foundation for the Jewish faith is the law. Leave out Jesus Christ and you have no foundation or cornerstone for the building.

God isn't in a hurry, so we must follow Abraham's example and have "faith and patience"

One of the first "symptoms" that Christians are not growing in the Lord is the feeling that they have "lost their salvation." In my own ministry, I have counseled with many people who either were sure they had never been saved or else certain that they had lost their salvation. I usually began with, "Tell me about your prayer life, your Bible reading and your Bible study," and the response would usually be an embarrassing silence. Prayer is to the inner person what breathing is to the body, and feeding on the Word is like eating a nourishing meal. How would we feel if we stopped breathing and eating? Once my counselees had confessed their sins of laziness and neglect, they regained their confidence in the Lord and the assurance of their salvation. The original audience of the epistle to the Hebrews hadn't apostatized and denied the Lord. The word used in Hebrews 6:6 means "to fall away." They were on a detour and needed to get back to the main road.

The writer of Hebrews used the metaphors of building (Heb. 6:1–3) and farming (6:7–8) to illustrate his point, and these two images fit perfectly into the history of Israel. Why go back to the Jewish faith when Jesus said that the temple you admire will be destroyed? The farm metaphor reminds us of our Lord's parable of the seeds and the soils (see Matt. 13:1–10, 18–23) and Isaiah's description of the Jewish "vineyard" in Isaiah 5:6: "I will make it a wasteland . . . and briars and thorns will grow there." The Jewish nation had no king or priest, yet in Jesus Christ we have both the true King and great High Priest. So why desert Him? "For the Israelites will live many days without king or prince, without sacrifice or sacred stones, without ephod or household gods" (Hos. 3:4).

If we are truly born again and therefore sealed by the Holy Spirit (see Eph. 1:13–14), it's impossible to "lose our salvation," but it is possible to live in such a way that we bring disgrace to the name of Jesus and feel like we don't belong to God's family. A believer out of fellowship with the Lord can do more damage to God's work than can an unbeliever (see Prov. 25:26). We all need diligence, faith and patience so we can claim our inheritance and not lose the blessing (see Heb. 6:11–12). Come to the throne of grace!

Dependability—The God of All Grace (Hebrews 6:13–20)

Diligence in the spiritual life leads to confidence in God and His Word. The readers of this epistle didn't need to go back to Judaism but to move ahead, trusting the God of Abraham, Isaac and Jacob, the God and Father of our Lord Jesus Christ. God kept His promises to Abraham, and He will keep His promises to us. Like Abraham, we don't always know where God is leading us (see Heb. 11:8), but like Abraham we can trust His promises. He doesn't always fulfill His promises immediately because God isn't in a hurry, so we must follow Abraham's example and have "faith and patience" (6:12). We can trust the character of God; it never changes. "I the Lord do not change" (Mal. 3:6). God sealed His promise to Abraham with an oath, and His oath is dependable (Heb. 6:16–18). God cannot lie, and His oath cannot be broken.

The writer closed this section with three pictures that depict confidence and security. The first is the Old Testament city of refuge (6:18), to which the people fled who had accidentally slain someone (Num. 35; Josh. 21). They could remain there and be protected from the victim's family members who might want to avenge the death. When the high priest died, the fugitive was permitted to return home in safety. Jesus is our refuge, and He is the High Priest who will never die (Heb. 7:16, 23–25). This means we are saved and kept by Him forever! We have the hope of "going home" to heaven, and therefore we ought to be encouraged.

The second picture is that of the anchor (6:19). The Greek Stoic philosopher Epictetus said, "One must not tie a ship to a single anchor, nor life to a single hope." But we who trust Jesus Christ have tied our hope to Him alone for He is "Christ Jesus our hope" (1 Tim. 1:1; and see Col. 1:5). The anchor of a boat goes downward to the seabed, but the anchor of God's church goes upward to heaven where Jesus is. A boat is anchored to keep it from drifting (see Heb. 2:1–4), but we are anchored *so that we might make progress!* Let us go on!

The third picture is that of the "forerunner" (6:20), the one who goes before and makes it possible for others to follow. The word was used of soldiers who went ahead of the army to open the way for them. The Old Testament high priest was definitely not a "forerunner" because nobody was permitted to follow him into the Holy of Holies. When Jesus died, the veil of the temple was torn in two from top to bottom (Matt. 27:50–51); His death was the final sacrifice that opened the way so that all His people might follow. Because of this new and living way, we can come into His presence at any time (Heb. 10:19–20), and we can be sure of being with Him in the place He is preparing for us in heaven (John 14:1–6).

Those believers who worry about "losing" their salvation should consider God's unchanging character, God's oath, the city of refuge, the anchor and the forerunner. They all speak of the confidence and security that maturing Christians enjoy.

Moses and Maturity

In the book of Genesis, the Israelites were simply another family in the land of Canaan, with Jacob as their head. Then Jacob and his family relocated to Egypt as special guests of Joseph and the Pharaoh, because Joseph had saved Egypt during its famine. In Egypt the Jews multiplied and became a mighty nation. But by then the Egyptians had forgotten both the famine and Joseph, and the new pharaoh enslaved the Jewish people. At the Exodus God delivered Israel, and they went out of Egypt in glorious freedom. That was easy compared to Moses' next task, which was to trust God to help him transform a nation of slaves into a free people who would worship and serve Him and conquer the land of Canaan.

I think it was the well-known Scottish preacher George Morrison who said, "It took one night to get Israel out of Egypt, but forty years to take Egypt out of Israel." As millions of tourists discover year by year, a change in geography doesn't alter the human heart. Husbands and wives as well as parents and children can argue in London and Paris as well as at home. In spite of all that God had done for Israel, as the people marched from the Red Sea to Sinai, they complained to Moses and said they wanted to go back to Egypt! This was an experience they repeated several times. But why would a free nation, being led by the Lord God, want to return to slavery? *Because in Egypt they had food and security and had no important decisions to make, while in the wilderness they had to trust God and live by His Word.* They had gotten accustomed to their slavery and learned to live with it, and as a result were totally unprepared to enter Canaan and conquer their enemies.

Jesus wants us to know the truth, because only the truth can set us free (John 8:31–32). Yet in many churches there are multitudes of immature people who fear freedom and want to remain babies and have others take care of them and tell them what to do. To these fearful immature people, the bondage of legalism is preferred to the dangers and demands of freedom. Israel had a very difficult time moving out of slavery and into freedom, and an entire generation had to die off before the nation was ready to enter the Promised Land and claim their inheritance.

When Israel was out of Egypt three months, Moses brought the people to Sinai where they camped for about two years. There God revealed His power and glory and gave them His law. It wasn't an easy experience for the Jews, for even Moses said, "I am trembling with fear" (Heb. 12:21). Freedom doesn't mean doing whatever we please and escaping the consequences. That's anarchy, and it never leads to maturity. Freedom means life controlled by truth and motivated by love, and nobody has a right to exercise authority who isn't under authority. At Sinai, Israel learned what all of God's people must learn: God is holy; His will is the expression of His love; and faith and obedience are the essentials for success in life. God disciplines us because He loves us and wants us to grow up, as we will discover in Hebrews 12.

Before we can rejoice in victory, we must submit in humility.

At Sinai, Israel built the tabernacle, established the priesthood and learned how to worship the Lord. God's glorious presence in the tabernacle was at the very center of the camp, and the Jewish people learned how to break camp in an orderly manner without asking, "Who is first?" Each tribe had its place both in the camp and in the march. Maturing people live that way. God gave them a calendar to follow and insisted that they follow it. They had to learn that God was in charge of their time as well as their possessions and their future.

Israel wasn't traveling to Canaan as tourists seeking entertainment. They were marching as an army, equipped by the Lord to be conquerors and take possession of their inheritance. They were learning the meaning of living by faith and obeying the

Word of God. Like infants in a family, Israel began their national life pampered and protected, but there came a time when they had to learn to respect God's authority and obey His orders.

The generation that died in the wilderness had been rebellious and self-centered, and they could never have conquered Canaan. Before we can be successful leaders and conquerors, we must first be obedient followers. Before we can rejoice in victory, we must submit in humility. Even Joshua had to learn that he was second in command (see Josh. 5:13–15)!

The writer of the book of Hebrews wanted his readers—and that includes us—to move from infancy to maturity, and this is not an easy experience. Joseph learned submission and obedience in an Egyptian prison, and Moses matured during forty years of shepherding in Midian. Joshua began as Moses' servant before receiving Moses' mantle, and David grew up during those years of exile in the Judean wilderness when King Saul pursued him. Even our Lord Jesus Christ "learned obedience from what he suffered" (Heb. 5:8). Dr. D. Martyn Lloyd-Jones said to me one day, "It's a sad thing when people succeed before they're ready for it." An old adage says, "Too much too soon means too bad."

The spiritual resources for maturity are available, so let's move to our next challenge: Let's go up!

5

Reality—Let's Go Up!

Depending on Heaven's Resources
Hebrews 7–10

Set your minds on things above, not on earthly things.
Colossians 3:2

The doctor delayed my surgery a few days because my pancreatic count was too high, and to alleviate my pain he gave me a combination of pain killers that made me hallucinate. Frequently I saw large psychedelic spiders scuttling about the room. More than once I tried to smash them with a rolled up newspaper, but they were immortal. My wife kept reminding me that there were no spiders in the room, but those spiders were as real to me as the room itself and the people in it.

In part 1 of his "Four Quartets," poet T.S. Eliot says, "Human kind cannot bear very much reality." This helps to explain the popularity of such distractions as alcohol and other narcotics, loud mindless music and "virtual" entertainment. I like what Elwood P. Dowd says to the psychiatrist in Mary Chase's award-winning play *Harvey*: "Doctor, I wrestled with reality for forty years, and I am happy to say that I finally won out over it." He got the victory over reality by inventing a six-foot white rabbit as his constant companion—and he ended up counseling the psychiatrist!

Heavenly Perspective

What is reality? Is it only what we encounter with our five senses? Were the multicolored spiders real because I saw them, or were they only medically induced electric currents in my brain? If I had continued to see those spiders after my surgery and recovery, my surgeon would have suggested I visit a psychiatrist who could help bring me back to reality. "The life that is neurotic or psychotic," writes H.A. Overstreet, "is one that has linked itself to an environment not really there: its responses are to fantasies and illusions."[1]

"An environment not really there . . ." Many people think this is a description of the Christian life because Christians hold to concepts and assurances that the world can't grasp. However, that accusation is an old one. Our Lord's family thought He was beside Himself (Mark 3:20–22), and the religious leaders in Jerusalem said that Jesus was "raving mad" (John 10:19–20). Of course, we would disagree with both groups. Most people in Jesus' time couldn't understand that He was in touch with a spiritual world that He loved and enjoyed but was a mystery to unbelievers. Even a brilliant man like Nicodemus couldn't grasp it with his natural intelligence. He first had to be born again (see John 3:1–15).

What kept Abraham going? Abraham had spiritual senses that kept him going. Seeing by faith the city that God was preparing for him (see Heb. 11:8–10). His pagan neighbors didn't see it. Moses "saw him who is invisible" (Heb. 11:27), and that kept him from being distracted by the so-called "real things" around him. When I was a seminary student, the distinguished Bible teacher Vance Havner preached in a chapel service, and I will never forget his statement based on Hebrews 11:24–29: "Moses saw the invisible, Moses chose the imperishable, and Moses did the impossible." Was Moses neurotic or psychotic—or something else altogether?

And what about the apostle Paul? While Paul was giving his defense before Portius Festus, the Roman procurator of Judea, the man shouted out, "You are out of your mind, Paul! . . . Your great learning is driving you insane" (Acts 26:24). Festus wasn't the only person to tell Paul he was crazy (2 Cor. 5:13). In the early days of evangelist D.L. Moody's ministry in Chicago, some of the newspapers called him "Crazy Moody." I hope those journalists lived long enough to discover how wrong they were. Moody wasn't crazy; he saw by faith what others couldn't see.

The recipients of this Hebrew letter were tempted to go back to traditional Judaism because it was a "real" religion. Their five senses told them so. They could see the temple with its busy priests and Levites, they could hear the psalms and they could talk to the other worshipers. Judaism had a religious calendar to follow and a remarkable history to admire. People brought real sacrifices to the temple and offered them on the altar to the Lord.

Their religion had come from God through Moses and no other religion could compare with it. The idol-worshiping Gentiles sneeringly asked, "Where is their God?" But the Jews knew the answer: "Our God is in heaven; he does whatever pleases him" (Ps. 115:1–3). But to the Jewish people reading the epistle to the Hebrews, it seemed reasonable to escape persecution by going back to their former "real" religion, *but everything "real" they wanted to return to would be destroyed in a few years!* After 70 AD, there would be no temple or priesthood or sacrifices; in fact, the Jewish people themselves would be scattered or slain, and their holy city would be destroyed.

There are many important things in life that we can't see, measure or weigh, but they are still just as real as the Washington Monument or the Egyptian Sphinx. Can you put dedication or honesty into a test tube and measure them in a laboratory? Is there a scientific formula for discovering if a man and woman really love each other? How do you mathematically categorize faith, hope or love? It bothers me when I see a sign that reads "Home for Sale" when it should say "House for Sale." You can build a home or wreck it, but you can't sell it. *The things we can see are precious to us because of the things we can't see!* Someone has well said, "It's good to have the things money can buy, provided you don't lose the things money can't buy." The things money can't buy are real but often invisible, yet they give value and substance to the visible things of life. Stop and think about that. How does the "invisible" rank in your life?

We don't look at heaven from earth's point of view; that's unbelief. We look at earth from heaven's point of view,

---

This brings us to Hebrews 7 through 10, the description of the possessions and privileges we Christians have because we are citizens of the heavenly spiritual world that today is invisible to our eyes but not to our faith. Everything really important to God's people is heavenly, and we can't see it with our physical eyes. We share in a heavenly calling (see Heb. 3:1) and have received the heavenly gift of salvation (6:4). We shall live forever in a heavenly country (11:16) and the heavenly Jerusalem (12:22). Our Father is in heaven (see Matt. 5:16), our citizenship is in heaven (see Phil. 3:20) and our names are recorded as the citizens of heaven (see Luke 10:20). Our treasures should be in heaven (see Matt. 6:20) because our inheritance is there (1 Pet. 1:4) and so is our reward (Luke 6:23). Our hope is in heaven (Col. 1:5), and Jesus is that hope (1 Tim. 1:1). Paul wrote, "I pray that the eyes of your heart may be enlightened" (Eph. 1:18), and we need to pray that prayer as well.

These blessings and more are ours because we have in heaven a *great High Priest* (Heb. 7) whose His ministry is based on a *better covenant* (Heb. 8) and carried out in a *more perfect sanctuary* (Heb. 9). Those who have trusted Him possess these blessings because of *the final and complete better sacrifice Jesus made for our sins* (Heb. 10). If these chapters teach us anything, it's that everything we need has been provided by the Lord, and we can have confidence in Him. Why go back to an earthly sanctuary that will be destroyed? Why submit to a covenant that has already grown old and is "obsolete and aging" (8:13)? Why worship in a sanctuary that is temporary and only a copy of the original sanctuary in heaven? Why depend on ineffective animal sacrifices offered by imperfect priests who will one day die? How foolish it is to replace the eternal with the temporary!

If you know what Jesus did on earth and trust Him as Lord and Savior, then you can be sure you are going to heaven; if you know what Jesus is doing for you now in heaven, you can be sure of His help as you live for Him here on earth. Jesus has entered into heaven "on our behalf" (6:20) and has opened for us "a new and living way" (10:20). We have "a great priest over the house [family] of God" (10:21); He cannot fail, and He will never die. No wonder Paul wrote, "Since, then, you have been raised with Christ, set your hearts on things above, where Christ is seated at the right hand of God. Set your minds on things above, not on earthly things" (Col. 3:1–2). We don't look at heaven from earth's point of view; that's unbelief. We look at earth from heaven's point of view, fixing "our eyes on Jesus, the author and perfecter of our faith" (Heb. 12:2). That's faith! That's living according to "the things above."

Just as we must develop our physical senses so we can function in the natural world, so we must develop our spiritual senses (see Heb. 5:14) so that the Spirit can enable us to function in the spiritual world, the "heavenly realms" that Paul wrote about (Eph. 1:3, 20; 2:6; 3:10; 6:12). We should exercise our spiritual sense of sight that enables us to see truth in God's Word and to recognize the hand of God at work in the everyday affairs of life (Heb. 11:13–16, 27; Ps. 119:18; 2 Cor. 4:16–18; Eph. 1:18; Acts 27:9–25). We also have a spiritual sense of taste to help us discern and enjoy what is really important (Heb. 6:4–5; Ps. 34:8; 119:103), and a sense of hearing so we can hear and understand the Word of God (Heb. 3:7, 15; 4:7; Matt. 13:9–17).

Jesus admonishes us to take heed *that* we hear (Matt. 13:9, 43), take heed *what* we hear (Mark 4:24) and take heed *how* we hear (Luke 8:18). We exercise our spiritual senses as we worship and serve the Lord, meditate on His Word and obey Him. This is how we grow in discernment (Heb. 5:11–14).

But a word of caution here: just because our citizenship and "real world" are in heaven, we aren't supposed to ignore our responsibilities on earth. D.L. Moody used to say, "Some Christians are so heavenly minded they are no earthly good." Good Christians will be good husbands and wives, good parents and children, good students and teachers, good workers and good citizens because they have heavenly senses and a heavenly perspective guiding their lives. Keeping our attention and affection on things above gives us the enlightenment and enablement we need in order to conquer the Enemy with his illusions and serve the Lord effectively. Like Jesus, if we are empowered by the Spirit, we will go "around doing good" (Acts 10:38).

Now let's consider the possessions and privileges God's people have because Jesus is alive and ministering in heaven. Remember, this heavenly world becomes more real to us than the world around us as we allow God's Spirit to teach us and empower us.

We Have a Great High Priest (Hebrews 7)

As we learned in the first chapter of our study, Jesus is at work in heaven today, ministering to and for His people. He not only has saved us, but He keeps us saved and keeps us safe as we walk with Him. He helps us claim our inheritance and equips us for life and service (Heb. 13:20–21). But our Lord couldn't serve as a priest if He were here on earth, because He belonged to the tribe of Judah and not to the priestly tribe of Levi. However, His priesthood doesn't come through Levi or Aaron, but from a man named Melchizedek who is mentioned twice in the Old Testament (Gen. 14:18; Ps. 110:4) and eight times in the book of Hebrews (5:6, 10; 6:20; 7:1, 10, 11, 15, 17). I suggest you pause now and read Genesis 14 and then Psalm 110.

After Abraham rescued Lot and his family from the four invading kings, he returned home and was met by the king of the wicked city of Sodom, who offered him all the spoils of battle as his reward. But Abraham wasn't for sale. Not wanting to harm his testimony and desiring only to glorify God, Abraham refused the offer and instead accepted the bread and wine from Melchizedek. He also gave Melchizedek a tithe of the spoils of battle. This entire episode is alive with spiritual truths, but I want to focus on Melchizedek as a type of Jesus Christ in His heavenly priesthood.

The Law of Moses separated the offices of priest and king, and if a king tried to take over the priesthood, God judged him (2 Chron. 26:16–23). But the offices of king and priest were united in Melchizedek, and they are united in Jesus Christ. As king, Jesus has supreme authority and power, and as priest, He has sympathy and grace. As king, Jesus gives us the authority and power we need for life and service, and as priest, He forgives us when we fail and encourages us when we need help. If we don't come to His throne for grace and mercy, we can't adequately live for Him here on earth. God's old covenant people *had* a priesthood, but God's new covenant people *are* kings and priests (Rev. 1:6), a holy and royal priesthood like that of Melchizedek (1 Pet. 2:5, 9).

The fact that Abraham, the father of the Jewish nation, gave tithes to Melchizedek shows how great Melchizedek really was. Abraham honored him, and Melchizedek blessed Abraham. "And without doubt the lesser is blessed by the greater" (Heb. 7:7). But the main point is that this ancient priest-king points to our Lord Jesus Christ, beginning with his name which means "king of righteousness." He was also king of Salem, which means "peace" (7:1–2). It's the Hebrew word *shalom.*

What a description of Jesus Christ! Because of faith in His finished work on the cross, we stand righteous before God (justified) and have peace with God (Rom. 5:1). Our Lord's sacrifice enabled "righteousness and peace [to] kiss each other" (Ps. 85:10). There can be no peace without righteousness: "The fruit of that righteousness will be peace; its effect will be quietness and confidence forever" (Isa. 32:17, and note James 3:17–18).

As far as the biblical record is concerned, Melchizedek experienced neither birth nor death (Heb. 7:3), and this typifies Jesus Christ, the eternal Son of God. Jesus "remains a priest forever" (7:3) and has been "made perfect forever" (7:28). He ministers "on the basis of the power of an indestructible life" (7:16). Unlike the Levitical priests, Jesus cannot die, and therefore He needs no successor. So important is our Lord's priestly ministry that the Father confirmed it with an oath (7:20–22; Ps. 110:4), something He didn't do when Aaron was ordained.

We must begin every day affirming that God is for us and not against us, and that Jesus is interceding for us at all times. You may know how exasperating it can be at your computer, telephone in hand, waiting for a technician. If only you could chat about your problem with a live human being instead of with an answering machine! But our connection with heaven isn't like that at all. "Before they call I will answer; while they are still speaking I will hear" (Isa. 65:24). The way to the throne of grace is open to us, and we are privileged to go there and open our hearts to our sympathetic High Priest.

We Have a Better Covenant (Hebrews 8)

"Jesus has become the guarantee of a better covenant" (Heb. 7:22).

Stop and think about the importance of covenants in contemporary life. Marriage is a covenant, the incorporation of a business is a form of covenant, and even the U.S. Constitution and the Bill of Rights are kinds of covenants. God made covenants with Noah (Gen. 9), Abraham (Gen. 12, 15, 17), Israel (Deut. 27–30) and David (2 Sam. 7), all of which guaranteed what He would do for His people; and He has always kept His Word.

The word translated "guarantee" in Hebrews 7:22 means a person who guarantees the fulfillment of the covenant promises. Another word is "surety." For example, Judah promised his father Isaac that he would be surety for Benjamin and was willing even to become Joseph's slave in order to save the lad (see Gen. 43:8–44:34). As a part of the "eternal covenant" between the members of the Godhead, Jesus agreed to die for the sins of the world and bear the punishment that we ought to suffer. He rose again and returned to heaven with the wounds of the cross on His body, and now He represents us before the Father.

This new covenant was not negotiated the way human "covenants" are hammered out. There was no compromising of certain points until an agreement was reached. God alone established it, and God alone administers it. He is in complete control. If there were no covenant, sinners would be lost forever; but because of His gracious covenant, sinners can be saved forever.

Does God require perfect righteousness of us? Yes, He does, but Jesus, our Surety, fulfilled that righteousness (2 Cor. 5:17–21). Nobody could justly condemn Him of any sin. Does Satan accuse us of sin? Yes, he does, but our Surety silences him. "Who will bring any charge against those whom God has chosen? It is God who justifies. Who is he that condemns? Christ Jesus, who died—more than that, who was raised to life—is at the right hand of God and is also interceding for us" (Rom. 8:33–34). Jesus has redeemed us from the curse of the law (Gal. 3:13) so that the Lord will never arrest us, judge us, convict us or condemn us (Rom. 8:1–4). He may chasten us, but that's another matter that we will consider later.

In establishing the new covenant in His own blood, Jesus Christ has fulfilled the demands of the law for us. At Sinai the Jewish nation promised to obey God and said to Moses, "Everything the Lord has said we will do" (Exod. 24:3). But within a short time, they made an idol, built an altar and entered into a godless orgy in disobedience to the very law they had promised to obey (Exod. 32–33). Our eternal salvation isn't based on the promises that we make to God, promises we think we can keep. Our eternal salvation is based on the promises He has made to us *that He cannot and will not break.*

Our eternal salvation is based on the promises He has made to us that He cannot and will not break.

Our eternal salvation is founded on the better promises of the new covenant (Heb. 8:6), and our Surety, Jesus Christ, has kept those promises and fulfilled the will of God on our behalf. Note the repetition of the phrase "I will" in Hebrews 8:7–12, which is quoted from Jeremiah 31:31–34. Israel made a promise, "Everything the Lord has said we will do," but they didn't keep it. God's people today are saved not by promising to do good works but by believing God's promise of forgiveness because of the finished work of Christ. "For it is by grace you have been saved, through faith—and this not from yourselves, it is the gift of God—not by works, so that no one can boast" (Eph. 2:8–9).

Christian believers live under a new covenant that is administered by a perfect priest in a perfect place—heaven. Believers are guaranteed that their sins are forgiven and that they will one day live in heaven with Jesus, and Jesus is the Surety of that covenant. As we saw in Hebrews 8, Jesus is the perfect High Priest and cannot fail or die. The old covenant dealt primarily with controlling outward behavior while the new covenant involves the work of the Holy Spirit in changing our hearts (Heb. 8:10; 2 Cor. 3:1–3). The old covenant says, "You must!" while the new covenant says, "You shall—and God will help you do it!" The requirement of the law is "met in us, who do not live according to the sinful nature but according to the Spirit" (Rom. 8:4).

We Have a More Perfect Sanctuary (Hebrews 9)

The emphasis in the book of Hebrews is on the tabernacle and its services rather than on the temple, because the writer was addressing a pilgrim people. Israel's tabernacle was built and furnished by the gifts and labors of the people according to the pattern God gave to Moses on Mount Sinai (Heb. 8:3–5; Exod. 25:9, 40). Moses didn't call a meeting of the elders and discuss what kind of sanctuary they should build or how they should worship God. God gave Moses the blueprint, and he had to follow it exactly. If God gave regulations for worship (Heb. 9:1) to His old covenant people, isn't it reasonable that He should give regulations for worship to His new covenant people? However, our world today looks more like the time of the judges, with everyone doing whatever seems fit in their own eyes (see Judg. 17:6; 18:1; 19:1; 21:25). More about this later.

There is a heavenly sanctuary, the "greater and more perfect tabernacle," that God designed and built in heaven without the aid of man. It belongs to the new creation, not the old creation (Heb. 9:11). Once a year on the Day of Atonement, the high priest of Israel sacrificed a goat and took its blood from the altar at the front of the tabernacle, through the outer court and into the holy place. Then he pulled back the veil and went into the Holy of Holies where the ark of the covenant and the cherubim were. He sprinkled the blood on the golden mercy seat that covered the ark, and God accepted the sacrifice and cleansed Israel. (Lev. 16). This sacrifice was imperfect and had to be repeated every year in contrast to the once-and-for-all perfect sacrifice of Jesus, the Lamb of God.

The Old Testament high priest went through the first two parts of the tabernacle into the Holy of Holies with the blood of a goat. Jesus, our great High Priest, passed through the heavens (Heb. 4:14) to present His own blood for the sins of the world. The earthly sanctuary pointed to something in heaven far greater than either the tabernacle or the temple (9:11–14). The Holy of Holies was not open to the people, and the high priest could enter it only once a year. But we who have trusted Jesus Christ can enter the Holy of Holies *in heaven* at any time and present our worship and petitions at the throne of grace. What a privilege!

There is no temple for worship in the heavenly city, for the whole city is a temple. (Rev. 21:22).[2] When you read the first half of the book of the Revelation, you discover "furnishings" in heaven that parallel those in the earthly sanctuary constructed by Moses. Hebrews 9:23 calls the earthly tabernacle furnishings "copies of the heavenly things."

The earthly tabernacle (*Exodus*)	*The heavenly sanctuary* (*Revelation*)
The Holy of Holies	The throne of God (4:1–2)
The candlestick	The seven lamps (4:5)
The bronze laver	The sea of glass (4:6)
Cherubim over the mercy seat	Living creatures before the throne (4:6–8)
Priests and Levites serving	Elders and angels serving (4:4, 9–11)
A brazen altar for sacrifices	An altar (6:9–11)
An incense altar	An incense altar (8:3–5)
The ark of the covenant	Ark of the covenant (11:19)

Our heavenly high priest is the perfect Son of God whose sacrifice of His own blood accomplished what the blood of animals could never accomplish. (That's the theme of Hebrews 10.) The earthly priests all exercised a temporary ministry, but Christ's ministry is eternal (Heb. 9:9–14). Our Lord's heavenly ministry isn't an external ritual like Israel's Day of Atonement, for He reaches into our inner person and cleanses the conscience (9:11–14); nor is it only for the church collectively, but for each individual believer. On the annual Day of Atonement, the people of Israel looked forward to the priest coming out of the tabernacle to bless them, and the church today looks forward to Jesus coming in glory. Note the repetition of the word "appear" in Hebrews 9:23–28: He appeared once to die for our sins (9:26), He appears now in heaven before God (9:24), and He shall appear a second time to take us to heaven (9:28).

Why go back to the copies on earth when we have the originals in heaven? Why focus only on ourselves instead of fixing our eyes on Jesus (Heb. 12:2)?

We Have a Final and Complete Sacrifice (Hebrews 10:1–19)

We have a perfect priest in heaven who serves in a perfect sanctuary, fulfilling a perfect covenant that is valid because of a perfect sacrifice *that never needs to be repeated.* "He sacrificed for their sins once for all when he offered himself" (Heb. 7:27). That sacrifice is described in Hebrews 10 and is contrasted with the old covenant sacrifices. If churches would take this chapter to heart, they would do away with the unbiblical practices that deny what this chapter teaches, traditions that hide the simple fact that salvation is by grace through faith.

The chapter begins with the reaffirmation that the tabernacle matters discussed so far are but "shadows" or copies of the spiritual realities in heaven (10:1; 9:23–24; 8:5). Moses was not to copy the heathen temples but the heavenly realities God had revealed to him on the mount. Evil King Ahaz made changes in the Jewish temple furnishings and nobody opposed him. He even commanded Uriah the high priest to replace the divinely ordained altar with a pagan altar he had seen in Damascus, and Uriah obeyed (2 Kings 16:10–20). This has a contemporary ring to it as churches today copy the world.

Animal blood can never wash away sin (Heb. 10:4), but the blood of Jesus takes away sin (John 1:29; 1 John 1:7). The priest could offer ceremonial forgiveness (Lev. 4:20, 26, 31), but Jesus gives internal cleansing and renewal to the heart and conscience (Heb. 10:11–18, 22). The old covenant sacrifices were repeated day after day, year after year, but Jesus died "once for all" and the debt was paid. Take note of that phrase "once for all." Jesus didn't make a down payment and ask us to keep up the installments. Jesus paid it all! It is finished!

We have no record of animals volunteering to give their lives, but Jesus willingly laid down His life for the sins of the world (John 10:11, 15–18). Because of His finished work, "we have been made holy through the sacrifice of the body of Jesus Christ once for all" (Heb. 10:10). There were no chairs in the tabernacle, because the priests' work was never done. Jesus shouted

"It is finished" and returned to heaven to sit down at the right hand of the Father (Heb. 10:11–14; see also John 19:30; Heb. 1:3; Eph. 1:20–23). The work of salvation has been completed, and the result is that we have a "new and living way" to God. Let's take advantage of it (Heb. 10:19–25).

We Are to Encourage Each Other to Persevere in Faith (Hebrews 10:19–39)

Unless we "go up," we will be tempted to "go back." When the common people in the camp of Israel came to the tabernacle, they could get only as far as the brazen altar. The priests and Levites ministered in the courtyard and the holy place, and only the high priest could go behind the veil into the Holy of Holies, and only once a year. But God's people today "have confidence to enter the Most Holy Place [in heaven] by the blood of Jesus" (Heb. 10:19). That "new and living way" was opened, not just for important people like kings and prophets, but *for us* (10:20)! At Mount Sinai Moses warned the people not to draw near to the mount lest they die (Exod. 19:12–13, 20–25), but now that the veil has been torn in two, we are urged to exercise faith and draw near to the throne of grace where we may experience communion with the Lord and cleansing from Him. "Come near to God and he will come near to you" (James 4:8).

We ought to *live* in the Holy of Holies and not simply "visit" it when we have problems to solve or battles to fight. "Lord, you have been our dwelling place throughout all generations" (Ps. 90:1). "He who dwells in the shelter of the Most High will rest in the shadow of the Almighty" (Ps. 91:1). "For in the day of trouble he will keep me safe in his dwelling; he will hide me in the shelter of his tabernacle and set me high upon a rock" (Ps. 27:5). When the psalmists write about "the shadow of your wings," it's usually a reference to the wings of the cherubim in the Holy of Holies where God's glory dwelt (Ps. 36:7–8; 61:4; 63:2, 7; 91:1–4).

But we don't rush carelessly into God's presence; we take

time for examination, confession and cleansing. The Old Testament priest wouldn't have dared to enter the Holy of Holies without first offering the sacrifice for his own cleansing, and he and the other priests were in danger of death if they failed to wash frequently at the laver (Exod. 30:17–21; 1 John 1:5–10). "Let us draw near to God with a sincere heart in full assurance of faith, having our hearts sprinkled to cleanse us from a guilty conscience and having our bodies washed with pure water" (Heb. 10:22; see also Eph. 5:25–27; John 15:3; Ps. 119:9).

This is not an invitation to solitary holiness, because the writer goes on to say, "And let us consider how we may spur one another on toward love and good deeds. Let us not give up meeting together, as some are in the habit of doing, but let us encourage one another—and all the more as you see the Day approaching" (Heb. 10:24–25). If we go into God's presence and *get* a blessing—what Jesus called "remaining [abiding] in me" (John 15:1–8)—we should then go out to others and *be* a blessing. If we ignore the laver and the Holy of Holies—cleansing and communion—we will defile and discourage others instead of edifying and encouraging them. Whenever I hear a defeated believer say, "I didn't get anything out of the service," I want to ask, "Did you encourage anybody else to get something out of the service?" If we don't put ourselves into it, we're not likely to get anything out of it.

Corporate worship is essential to the spiritual health and ministry of believers individually and churches collectively. Worship means exalting the Lord, not entertaining the saints, and yet more and more we see sanctuaries becoming theaters and "worship leaders" performers. The schedule for the service looks like a script for a television program, complete with directions for lighting (colors and intensity), sound (intensity) and choreography. Yes, "everything should be done in a fitting and orderly way" (1 Cor. 14:40), and everything "must be done so for the strengthening of the church" (14:26). But it shouldn't be a Broadway production that precludes corporate participation.

The fact that Jesus died on the cross and paid the penalty of sin, that He completed the work of redemption and is ruling on His throne now should encourage us to love Him more and serve Him better. When we observe the Lord's Supper (the Eucharist or Communion), we celebrate His past victory on the cross, our present experience of fellowship with Jesus and His people and the future blessed hope "until he comes" (1 Cor. 11:26). The important thing isn't *where* we meet together, whether in an ornate cathedral or a private home, but *that* we meet together, and that our meeting glorifies Jesus Christ alone.

"Let us draw near to God with a sincere heart. . . . Let us hold unswervingly to the hope we profess. . . . And let us consider how we may spur one another on toward love and good deeds" (Heb. 10:22–24). Jesus cried, "It is finished" (John 19:30), and because of that, we keep on going. This is true reality.

6

Ministry—Let's Go Out!

Serving Jesus in a Needy World
Hebrews 11–13

Let us, then, go to him [Jesus] outside the camp,
bearing the disgrace he bore.
Hebrews 13:13

As Christian believers, we claim our inheritance, mature in our faith and fellowship at the throne of grace in heaven, not just for our own enjoyment but that we might serve and glorify God. Selfish Christianity is not biblical Christianity. The church of Jesus Christ exists for others, not for itself, and the emphasis must be on *involvement* and not on *enjoyment*.

The church is a spiritual body and each member is gifted, not only for service *to* the body but also for service *through* the body to a needy world. "You are the light of the world," said Jesus. "Let your light shine before men, that they may see your good deeds and praise your Father in heaven" (Matt. 5:14, 16). Whether we are working in the marketplace or worshiping in the sanctuary, we must do everything as to the Lord. "So whether you eat or drink or whatever you do, do it all for the glory of God" (1 Cor. 10:31).

The believers who first received the epistle to the Hebrews were considering abandoning this basic truth. They were looking for a religion that would protect them from persecution and give them acceptance in society. They wanted to return to the synagogue as pious Jews but not as witnesses for Jesus Christ. That way they could enjoy a religion that was safe, comfortable and respectable—not unlike the kind of Christianity we see in many churches today. It's much easier to "go to church" (a building) than to "be the church" (a body) in our needy world. These Hebrew believers forgot that Jesus was cast out of the synagogue in his hometown of Capernaum (Luke 4:1–30) and that at least one of His converts was thrown out of a synagogue in Jerusalem (John 9:34–38). The apostle Paul and his co-workers were often driven not only out of the synagogues but also out of the cities (Acts 13:46–52; 14:1–6; 17:1–9).

The strategy of some churches today is similar to that of those first-century Jewish believers: to imitate the world in order to attract the world; to make Christianity easy to accept. But the truth is just the opposite: it's because Christians are different from others that we attract others. If you are odd, you repel people; if you are different, you attract them. Jesus never promised us lives of safety and comfort. Following Him means taking up a cross, and the cross implies suffering and death. "If you belonged to the world, it would love you as its own. As it is, you do not belong to the world, but I have chosen you out of the world. That is why the world hates you. . . . If they persecuted me, they will persecute you also" (John 15:19–20).

When he wanted to describe the Christian's true spiritual location in this world, the writer of the Hebrews used the word "outside." The sin offering was taken "outside the camp" and burned. Jesus suffered and died "outside the city gate," rejected by His own people. God's people are supposed to "go to him outside the camp, bearing the disgrace he bore" (Heb. 13:11–13). To a devout Jew, "outside the camp" meant defilement and disgrace. Outside the camp was where the lepers and other unclean people lived (Lev. 13:46; Num. 5:1–4). Criminals were slain outside the camp (Lev. 24:14), and human excrement was deposited there (Deut. 23:12–14). You wouldn't find the most expensive and exclusive real estate outside the camp.

But that's where Gods expects to find us. Why? Because that's where Jesus went, and that's where Jesus is! "Let us, then, *go to him* outside the camp, bearing the disgrace he bore" (Heb. 13:13). Whatever we do for the lost, the poor, the rejected and the needy, we do for Jesus (Matt. 25:31–46). Every Christian believer and every Christian congregation is supposed to go outside the camp and be involved in ministry to people who need them, and the last three chapters of Hebrews explain what this ministry means. We can summarize it in these three statements: True faith leads to obedience (Heb. 11). Obedient faith requires endurance (Heb. 12). Faith, obedience and endurance can lead to effective witness (Heb. 13).

True Faith Leads to Obedience (Hebrews 11)

This chapter makes it clear that people have always been saved by faith and have proved their faith by their obedience to the Lord. This doesn't mean they were perfect, any more than believers today are perfect, but it does mean they gave evidence of their faith by their works. "What good is it, my brothers, if a man claims to have faith but has no deeds? Can such faith save him?" (James 2:14). That question can be translated, "Can that kind of faith save them?" The answer, of course, is no. The only kind of faith that saves is the faith that leads to obedience and enables us to serve God and please Him. Believing God means doing His will in spite of the feelings within us, the circumstances around us or the consequences before us. With that definition in mind, take time to read Hebrews 11 and see if it doesn't fit.

Faith is only as good as its object. Put your faith in your experience, and you will get what experience can do for you. Put your faith in money, and you will get what money can accomplish. *Put your faith in Almighty God, and you will experience what God can do.* "For nothing will be impossible with God" (Luke 1:37, NASB). God commands us and backs up His command with His promise, and we believe His Word and act upon it. The result is that He is glorified by accomplishing His purposes in and through us. Faith is not an emotion that we work up but a confidence we have from the Lord because we rely on His Word and obey it.

Believing God means doing His will in spite of the feelings within us, the circumstances around us or the consequences before us.

According to verses 1–3 and 7 of Hebrews 11, *faith enables us to see.* No man or woman was present when God spoke the universe into existence, yet we who walk by faith see His grace, power and wisdom everywhere we look, and we can joyfully sing, "This is my Father's world." Noah never saw rain, yet he believed God and proved his faith by building the ark. Abraham and Sarah didn't know where they were going when they left Ur, yet they believed God and went out and ultimately arrived in Canaan. They didn't know how at that stage in life they could have a son, yet they believed God and He kept His promise. Moses didn't succeed because of his Egyptian education (Acts 7:22) but because of his living faith in the living God (Heb. 11:24–29).

Faith enables us to serve. Whether it's Abel worshiping, Enoch walking with God in an evil world, Noah building an ark, Abraham offering His only son Isaac on the altar, Moses confronting Pharaoh or leading Israel through the Red Sea on dry land, Joshua conquering a city, Gideon defeating a huge army with 300 soldiers or David facing Goliath with only a sling—all of them did what they did by faith in God and to the glory of God.

If you want to update this list, then read church history. It was by faith that James Hudson Taylor started the China Inland Mission and saw multitudes trust Christ. It was by faith that Dwight L. Moody founded the Moody Bible Institute in Chicago, which since 1887 has trained thousands to serve the

Lord. It was by faith Fredrik Franson founded the Scandinavian Alliance Mission, now known as TEAM (The Evangelical Alliance Mission) with missionaries serving around the world. Time fails us to tell about Lottie Moon, Malla Moe, Bill Bright, Billy Graham, J. Irvin Overholtzer, Oswald J. Smith, Percy Crawford, Jack Wyrtzen, Corrie Ten Boom and many more, all of whom glorified God by trusting Him and obeying His will. They were motivated and energized by faith, not by fame, and God honored their faith with fruit—and still is honoring their faith.

Discouraged Christians live in the "past indelible" tense. Fearful Christians live in the "present impossible." But conquering Christians live in the "future invisible."

Along with seeing and serving, there's another facet to Christian ministry: *faith enables us to suffer.* Hebrews 11:35–39 tells about "others" who seemed to be failures. They didn't conquer cities or perform miracles, but they still served the Lord. The Greek New Testament has two words translated "others": *allos*, meaning "others of the same kind," and *heteros*, meaning "others of a different kind." (Our English word "heterodox" means "holding a different opinion.") These unnamed saints belonged to "others of a different kind." They sacrificed, suffered and even died for their faith, and yet God honored them as heroes of faith along with David and Joshua and the rest. During their ministries, they may have felt as though they had failed miserably, yet in God's sight, they were "more than conquerors" (Rom. 8:37) as much as the people named in the first thirty-four verses. "Therefore judge nothing before the appointed time; wait till the Lord comes" (1 Cor. 4:5).

There are three "tenses" in life, two of which must be avoided. Discouraged Christians live in the "past indelible" tense, forgetting that the victorious Christian life is a series of new beginnings. We need not be shackled by either the unchanging failures or the successes of the past. Fearful Christians live in the "present impossible," paralyzed by what they see and how they feel. But conquering Christians walk by faith and live in the "future invisible," like Abraham, Moses and Paul, and the creative Christians I named earlier. Problems are only opportunities to see what God can do as He transforms weakness into strength and poverty into plenty.

Most of us are good at thinking up excuses not to trust God, but the people you meet in Hebrews 11 will not accept excuses. Are you saying, "I'm too old to begin this journey of faith?" Don't tell that to Abraham and Sarah, who were seventy-five and sixty-five respectively when they left home for the land of promise. Or you may be saying, "I'm too young to live by faith." David was likely a teenager when he killed Goliath, and Isaac was just a young man when he willingly surrendered to be put on the altar. "But I don't have much talent," you argue. Gideon felt the same way, but the Lord transformed him from a fearful farmer into a victorious general. The prophet Jeremiah argued with God about his call because he felt he was too young and not able to speak well. "Before I formed you in the womb, I knew you," God replied; "before you were born I set you apart; I appointed you as a prophet to the nations" (Jer. 1:5). Jeremiah believed God, and his faith carried him through more than forty years of difficult and yet courageous ministry.

When I was serving in Youth for Christ International, Dr. Bob Cook used to remind us, "Keep your ministry on a miracle basis. If you can explain what's going on, God didn't do it." When we live and work by faith, we bring glory to God *because we can't take the credit.* Each new problem challenges us and each new victory humbles us. Dr. R.W. Dale, one of England's best-known preachers, visited some of D.L. Moody's meetings during Moody's Birmingham evangelistic campaign. He wrote about Mr. Moody that his "work was most plainly of God, for I could see no real relation between him and what he had done. He laughed cheerily, and said he should be very sorry if it were otherwise."[1]

"So faith comes from hearing, and hearing by the word of Christ" (Rom. 10:17, NASB). Believers who devote themselves to the Word of God and receive it into their inner being are the ones who grow in faith (Ps. 1:2). The Holy Spirit uses that Word to equip and enable them when the challenges come. "I used to think I should close my Bible and pray for faith," said D.L. Moody, "but I came to see that it was in studying the Word that I was to get faith." What we should do is pray for faith and then open our Bibles! "True faith," said Mr. Moody, "is man's weakness leaning on God's strength."

True Faith and Obedience Lead to Endurance (Hebrews 12)

The Christian life is a journey of faith. If we stand still too long, we eventually fall backward, but if, with God's help, we press forward, we mature in Christian character and accomplish what God has called us to do. John Bunyan's book *The Pilgrim's Progress from This World to That Which Is to Come* reminds us that God's people are pilgrims who should be making steady progress. (If you have never read Bunyan's classic, by all means do so, with your Bible at hand.) Our faith journey is difficult but it's not impossible, because the Lord will provide the endurance we need if we trust Him. "Being confident of this, that he who began a good work in you will carry it on to completion until the day of Christ Jesus" (Phil. 1:6).

The writer of Hebrews commended his readers because early in their Christian walk they had "endured in a great conflict full of suffering" and not given up (10:32). He then encouraged them in 10:36 "to persevere so that when you have done the will of God, you will receive what he has promised." Trusting God's promise, plus doing God's will plus, receiving the daily endurance God gives—equals accomplishing what God commanded and receiving what God promised.

The word translated "endurance" literally means "to remain under." It describes a person who is under extreme pressure, who is suffering and carrying burdens, and yet who courageously keeps going. "Not only so, but we also glory in our sufferings, because we know that suffering produces perseverance [endurance], perseverance, character; and character, hope" (Rom. 5:3–4). The word "endure" is used three times in Hebrews 12, twice describing the experience of Jesus in His suffering (12:2–3) and once the experience of suffering believers (12:7). Colossians 1:11 tells us that we can be "strengthened with all power according to his glorious might so that you may have great endurance and patience." We need patience to deal with difficult people and endurance to deal with difficult circumstances. (In the Greek, "patience" literally means "long tempered.") Quitters are not conquerors, and the believers described in Hebrews 11 were not quitters.

Now let's consider the chapter as a whole. In Hebrews 12 the writer gives us three instructions that, if we follow them by faith, will give us the endurance we need as we meet difficulties in our faith journey.

Look to Jesus by Faith (Hebrews 12:1–4)

The believers described in Hebrews 11 bear witness to us that the life of faith is both available and achievable and that God can be trusted to fulfill His promises. But the greatest witness of all is the Son of God who fought the greatest battles and paid the greatest price. Please keep in mind that when Jesus was ministering on earth, He didn't use His divine powers for Himself but lived by faith in the Father just as we must do today. He prayed and meditated on the Word daily. He yielded to the Spirit and obeyed the Father's will, and we should follow His example. Jesus is our faithful and sympathetic High Priest, and we can trust Him as we go "outside the camp" and minister to others.

The first image in this passage is that of Jesus the Pioneer (Heb. 12:2), a word that means "one who goes ahead, a leader who opens the way for others to follow." Personally, I'm not the pioneer type. I prefer somebody else to make the reservations and go ahead to set things up, and I'll be happy to come later. One of the problems of the church today is that people are too much like me: poor pioneers but happy settlers. If we follow Jesus, we must enter unknown territory in our ministries; otherwise, we're just maintaining the status quo. To go outside the camp demands the pioneer spirit that, like Abraham and Sarah, obeys even if we don't know where we're going.

"True faith," said Mr. Moody, "is man's weakness leaning on God's strength."

The second image in this passage is that of athletes who remove every hindrance so they can run easily and not be tripped up or held back. In the race of faith, a hindrance may not necessarily be a gross sin, but because it keeps us from doing our best, we must remove it. Almost anyone can choose between the good and the bad; the maturing believer must choose between the better and the best. Anything in our lives that hinders us from enjoying God's love, receiving God's power and obeying God's will is a hindrance to us, even though other Christians may be allowed to have it or do it. When I was a new believer, someone gave me a tract entitled "Others May, You Cannot," and its message really helped me. If we're going to win the race, we must look to Jesus by faith and not look at other runners and get our signals from them.

But it isn't enough just to be ready for the race. We must also fix our eyes on the goal and keep running until we get there. It takes perseverance and endurance to reach the goal, and if we become distracted by other runners or by the spectators in the stands, we will not win the race. Jesus is the "pioneer and perfecter of our faith," which means He prepares the way for us, starts us on the race and, if we trust Him, enables us to reach the goal. It isn't enough just to start well; we also need to finish well, and He enables us to do just that. "If only I may finish the race and complete the task the Lord Jesus has given me" (Acts 20:24). Paul achieved that aim, for he wrote at the close of his life, "I have fought the good fight, I have finished the race, I have kept the faith" (2 Tim. 4:7). We should daily be asking the Lord to help us finish well. In the Greek races there was only one first-place prize; those who came in second or third were not honored. In the Christian race, however, every believer may win the prize (1 Cor. 9:24–27).

In the ancient Greek races it was essential that the runners remain in their assigned lanes. To change lanes or to try to force another runner into a different lane was grounds for disqualification. Each of us in God's family is assigned a lane, a ministry to perform and a goal to achieve. The Lord will not compare us with other runners and judge us by what they accomplished; rather, we will be judged by how well we did with the gifts and opportunities He gave us. In ancient Greek races, like in races today, the athletes competed against each other. In the church of Corinth, some believers were cheering for Paul, others for Apollos and still others rooting for Peter, and Paul told them they were all wrong (1 Cor. 1:10–17). We are all runners, not spectators or cheerleaders, and we are to encourage each other, not compete with each other. We are competing with ourselves and not with others, because there should be no competition in the family of God.

What was it that helped to keep Jesus run the race? "For the joy set before him [he] endured the cross, scorning its shame (Heb. 12:2). What is that joy? It's the joy of one day presenting His bride, the church, to the Father in glory, without stain or fault (Jude 24). As He faced the cross, Jesus looked beyond the suffering to the glory the Father had promised Him (John 12:20–29; 13:1; 17:1–5). Jesus compared His Calvary experience to a woman giving birth to a baby (John 16:19–22); the same baby that gave her pain also brought her joy! As we serve the Lord, the trials of life that cause us pain today will one day bring us joy when we see the Lord. "I consider that our present sufferings are not worth comparing with the glory that will be revealed in us" (Rom. 8:18).

In order to endure the present sufferings, you have to keep focused on the goal. As Jesus fixed his eyes on the Father, we must fix our eyes on Jesus. To "fix our eyes on Jesus" doesn't mean creating an image in our mind of Jesus in some gospel situation and then meditating on that image. We don't know what Jesus looked like and it's wrong to manufacture "idols" in our minds. To "fix our eyes on Jesus" means to allow the Spirit to show us Jesus in the Word—what He said and did, how He responded to the needs of people, the promises He made and the power He revealed. It means realizing afresh our Lord's concerns for people and their needs and allowing the Spirit to apply this to our own lives as we meditate and pray. It means focusing on Jesus and not on the feelings within us, the circumstances around us or the consequences before us. This is why it's important that we know the Scriptures and commit passages to memory, because we may not be able to turn to the Bible and look up an appropriate verse.

In 1966 a drunken driver going at least eighty miles an hour crossed the yellow line and hit my car as I came around a curve. The crash almost killed me. In the ambulance, as the medics worked hard to keep me alive, one verse came to my mind and stayed there: "Great is the Lord, and greatly to be praised; and his greatness is unsearchable" (Ps. 145:3, KJV). *"The Lord is great in love,"* I thought to myself, *"so I don't have to be afraid because He is on the throne. He is great in power and will make all things work out for my good and His glory."* As I drifted in and out of consciousness, I focused on the greatness of God in Jesus and had a peace in my heart that wasn't caused by medication. The hospital chaplain told my wife that I wouldn't make it through the night, but he was wrong. Our great God saw us through.

Rest in the Father's Love (Hebrews 12:5–13)

The theme of this passage is child training, but most English translations use the word "discipline," which can mean different things to different people. Most of us think of discipline as punishment for disobedience, but in the ancient Greek world, it also meant the physical training of a child in exercise and athletics. The father would bring his young son to the gymnasium and put him under the authority of a trainer who would help the lad develop a sound mind and a sound body. The regimen wasn't easy, and no doubt at times the boy thought he was being punished, but that wasn't the goal at all. If there was any punishment applied, it was only for his good. If muscles aren't used, they atrophy, or wither away, and if faith isn't exercised, it grows weak. It takes discipline to maintain strength.

Like a good physician, the Lord may hurt us,
but He will never harm us.

Another type of discipline is the punishment kind. Sometimes a loving father will allow his child to fail at something in order to discipline the child to teach him or her the right path. Notice that the father disciplines his child and not other people's children. Likewise, the heavenly Father permits his children to go through difficult experiences so that we might mature and be able to face life courageously. When God disciplines you, it is proof that you are truly His child and that He loves you. People who profess to be saved yet persist in disobeying the Father and never suffer for it have never been born into God's family. "If you are not disciplined (and everyone undergoes discipline), then you are illegitimate children and not true sons" (12:8). Satan wants us to believe that our trials are evidence that we are not God's children, but it's quite the opposite. Because our Father loves us, He encourages us to obey and do better. He wants us to be mature children and not little babies.

How we respond in "God's gymnasium" will determine how we mature. We can make light of our trials and depend on our own strength; we can get discouraged and quit (12:5); or we can respect our Father and endure whatever He ordains for us (12:9), knowing that He loves us. When we surrender and obey, it leads to growth in holiness and "a harvest of righteousness and peace" (12:10–11). At the time, trials are not enjoyable, but the harvest brings joy and blessing that we could receive no other way. When you consider the blessings their trials brought to Joseph, Moses, David, Jeremiah, the apostles and even our Lord Jesus, you see how important it is to submit to the will of God. Like a good physician, the Lord may hurt us, but He will never harm us.

When we are hurting, the Enemy taunts us and says, "Your Father doesn't love you. If He loves you, He would never have permitted this to happen." But faith replies, "This pain is proof that He does love me and that He is working out His purpose in my life." God wants us to run the race successfully, and sometimes He uses affliction to "repair" and strengthen our spiritual joints and muscles so we can run like winners (12:12–13). In the Christian's life of faith, trials and pain don't punish us; they prepare us for what God wants to accomplish in and through us. An Olympic gold medalist doesn't start training a week before the event! If you are experiencing trials today, if you are suffering right now, rest in the fact that God is using this trial to strengthen you. He "works for the good of those who love Him, who have been called according to his purpose" (Rom. 8:28).

Enjoy Your Heavenly Blessings (Hebrews 12:18–28)

There is a sharp contrast between Israel's frightening experience at Mt. Sinai (Exod. 19:10–25; 20:18–21) and the church's happy fellowship in the "joyful assembly" of saints and angels in glory. When God approached the Israelites at Mt. Sinai, it was with great power that terrified the people. Only Moses could come before God. In heaven all the saints approach the living God joyfully and boldly. But this experience isn't simply a future hope; it's a present experience. "But you have come to Mount Zion" (Heb. 12:22). Jerusalem and the Jewish temple on Mount Zion are symbols of the heavenly Jerusalem (see Gal. 4:19–31; Ps. 2; 110:1–4). The patriarchs looked for this heavenly city (Heb. 11:10, 16) and are now in it, and one day we shall join them. Meanwhile, by faith we currently live "in the heavenlies"—the theme of Hebrews 7–10, "Let us go up"—and we enjoy the riches of God's grace and glory now. "Our citizenship is in heaven" (Phil. 3:20), and today we may enjoy all the privileges of that heavenly citizenship as we eagerly wait for the Lord to return. We don't live under the old covenant given at Sinai but under the new covenant now being mediated by our Lord Jesus Christ who is in heaven. I don't physically fellowship with the great men and women of faith in antiquity, but as I read the Word, their example and exhortation really does encourage me as I run the race.

The church's worship and fellowship on earth ought to be conducted in the same way that worship and fellowship is conducted in heaven. "Your will be done on earth as it is in heaven" (Matt. 6:10). The patterns for both the tabernacle and temple came from heaven, as did the instructions concerning the worship presented in these sanctuaries (Exod. 25:40; 1 Chron. 28:11–19; Heb. 8:5). This ought to motivate us to worship the Lord "with reverence and awe" (Heb. 12:28), rather than approach God casually as unbelievers do.

"See to it that you do not refuse him who speaks" (12:25). Notice that the verse is in the present tense. God is speaking to us today, and too many people just aren't listening. "Whoever has ears, let them hear what the Spirit says to the churches" is a statement so important that Jesus repeated it seven times (Rev. 2:7, 11, 17, 29; 3:6, 13, 22), and He also used the word "repent" seven times (2:5 [twice], 16, 21, 22; 3:3, 19). While we are encouraging the lost sinners to repent, let's not forget that individual Christians and churches also need to repent.

Some people teach that when Jesus was on earth, He was a prophet, that now in heaven He is a priest, and that one day He will return and establish a glorious kingdom on earth and His church shall reign with Him (Luke 22:29–30; Rev. 20:4–6). But Jesus is enthroned and reigning now (Eph. 1:20–23), and we already are citizens of His gracious kingdom, "a kingdom that cannot be shaken" (Heb. 12:28).

God is shaking things so that what doesn't belong in our lives and churches will fall away, and we will build on the eternal.

Wherever we look today, we see things shaking—governments, businesses, marriages, homes, contracts, treaties and institutions of one kind and another. The stock market shakes, leadership shakes, even the earth and the oceans shake and destroy cities without warning. God is shaking things! Why? The writer tells us: "so that what cannot be shaken may remain" (12:27). If our lives and churches are not built on Jesus Christ, the Word of God and prayer (Acts 6:4; 1 Cor. 3:10–15), they will not endure. Too many individuals and ministries are depending on the scaffolding and not the foundation, and that scaffolding will be destroyed when God shakes things. No matter how imposing our edifices or how large our crowds, unless we build on the heavenly, our works will be destroyed with the earthly. God is shaking things so that what doesn't belong in our lives and churches will fall away, and we will build on the eternal. Our heavenly blessing is to be able to come into the presence of the holy God and to be built on nothing less than Jesus Christ and His righteousness, to be built on an unshakable foundation. We must get rid of excuses and encumbrances and run the race with our eyes of faith fixed on Jesus. We must rest in God's love no matter how much we hurt, and we must keep our hearts and minds on the things of heaven as we serve on earth. We belong to an unshakable kingdom, and we must not be frightened or detoured by the rapid changes occurring in the church or in our lives. When the shaking is over, the best will be left behind. It's time to "go out," and Hebrews 13 tells us what is required for us to be effective.

True Faith, Obedience and Endurance Will Result in Witness for Christ (Hebrews 13)

True faith leads to obedience (Heb. 11), and true faith and obedience will supply the endurance we need to keep going (Heb. 12). But faith, obedience and endurance must be focused on ministry to others, and that's the basic theme of Hebrews 13. We are commanded to "go outside the camp" to where Jesus goes before us to prepare the way for our witness and service (13:13). Faith without obedience is dead, and obedient faith without endurance is temporary; but when faith, obedience and endurance work together, the combination is dynamic. These three elements enable us to accomplish great things for the Lord, just as the people in Hebrews 11 were honored for their faith. Why? Because when faith, obedience and endurance work together, they help to create a witness that God can use to convert people and expand the unshakable kingdom.

When we go outside the camp, unsaved people sense that we are different, and this discovery can produce a variety of responses: curiosity, suspicion, fear and often opposition. These people might welcome us or attack us, but they can't avoid us as long as our witness is valid. This witness will bring disgrace just as Jesus was disgraced (13:13). Regardless of how people respond to our witness, each contact can open a door of opportunity for us that might result in somebody trusting Christ.

It isn't necessary for us to manufacture clever artificial situations. Faith is living without scheming. Jesus has already gone before us to prepare the way and we simply "go to him outside the camp," yielding to His will. He uses us to share the gospel with others in the way He has planned. We need to be prepared so we can take advantage of our witnessing opportunities outside the camp. Hebrews 13 describes who and what we are as Christians and how we can be equipped to share Christ with people in Enemy territory. Let us go out!

We Are Saints—Let's Be Godly (Hebrews 13:12)

Jesus suffered "to make the people holy through his own blood" (13:12). What a powerful statement! "Jesus suffered" is history, "to make the people holy" is theology, and "let us go" is ministry based on history and theology, which is the only kind of witness worth giving. To "make holy" means to be set apart by God for His own exclusive purpose. It doesn't mean that we are sinless or that we never make mistakes. Another translation is "sanctified." Jesus said to the Father, "For them I sanctify myself, that they too may be truly sanctified" (John 17:19). The New Living Translation reads, "And I give myself entirely to you so they also might be entirely yours." So, as we join Jesus outside the camp, we must keep in mind that, as saints, we belong wholly to God and that He will care for us.

But we must be careful to *live* like God's people. What we are must match what we say, otherwise we have no real witness; and the world is quick to detect inconsistency. As we share the disgrace Jesus bore, the world will treat us the way they treated Him. They lied about Him ("He stirs up the people!"), slandered Him ("A drunkard! A glutton! A demonized man!") and rounded up false witnesses to condemn Him. Jesus didn't argue with His enemies; He simply did the Father's will and prayed for and died for those who hated Him.

This is why our chapter opens with some pointed admonitions about love (Heb. 13:1–6). If we don't love one another in the church family, how can we love the lost who are outside the family? If there isn't love in the home and purity in the marriage, how can we talk to sinners about Jesus? If we love money more than we love people, our witness will have no power. Real saints remember and respect their past spiritual leaders who pointed them to Christ (13:7–10), and they also obey their present leaders who faithfully "keep watch" over the flock (13:17). This is the best way to prevent us from foolishly accepting every false doctrine that comes our way (13:9–10).

We Are Outcasts—Let's Be Different (Hebrews 13:11–13)

One of the most popular philosophies of ministry today says that we should imitate, not offend, the people we're trying to reach. This may build enthusiastic crowds, but it doesn't always build godly New Testament churches. It doesn't sound like "bearing the disgrace he [Jesus] bore." In the first century you couldn't get any lower than to die on a cross, which explains Philippians 2:8: "He [Jesus] humbled himself by becoming obedient to death—even death on a cross." But modern religious people have turned the cross into a piece of expensive jewelry or a sedate monument in a cemetery. After all, who wants a religion of shame and disgrace? Yet Paul wrote, "I am not ashamed of the gospel, because it is the power of God for the salvation of everyone who believes" (Rom. 1:16).

Unless we compromise in some way, once we go outside the camp and identify with Christ, we are indelibly branded by the world as outcasts, like the "others" in Hebrews 11:35–38. Those believers were tortured, imprisoned, ridiculed, whipped, stoned, stabbed, mistreated, left destitute of food and shelter and forced to live in caves and holes in the ground. Yet the Bible says that "the world was not worthy of them" (11:38)! We don't seem to have many of these "worthies" in the churches of the Western world today.

"If anyone would come after me," Jesus said, "he must deny himself and take up his cross and follow me. For whoever wants to save his life will lose it, but whoever loses his life for me will find it" (Matt. 16:24–25). That's life with Jesus outside the camp. This doesn't imply that "outside the camp" refers exclusively to "lower class people" (whatever that means), because Jesus was persecuted and condemned by successful "upper class people" who had enviable reputations. "Is it not the rich who are exploiting you?" asked James. "Are they not the ones who are dragging you into court? Are they not the ones who are slandering the noble name of him to whom you belong?" (James 2:6–7).

Unless we compromise in some way, once we go outside the camp and identify with Christ, we are indelibly branded by the world as outcasts.

After preaching a courageous sermon against the current religious leaders, our Lord announced that the temple was desolate because God had abandoned it; and then He left the temple for the last time (Matt. 23:38–24:1). The people He preached against in Matthew 23 were the very ones who had Him arrested, tried in a "kangaroo court" and crucified like a criminal. "If they persecuted me," He told His disciples, "they will persecute you also" (John 15:20).

I have a Christian friend who was fired once for working too hard. He was a college student at the time and glad to have a job. His Christian work ethic was such that he made some of the other employees look bad, so the foreman fired him. I know other believers who have been passed by for promotions primarily because they were Christians. You may know believers who were in the armed forces and were persecuted because they didn't drink, swear, tell dirty stories, gamble or look for ways to get out of work. You may also know some families who are "overlooked" when the neighborhood gets together for a cookout. "But rejoice that you participate in the sufferings of Christ, so that you may be overjoyed when his glory is revealed" (1 Pet. 4:13).

We Are Pilgrims—Let's Focus on Heaven (Hebrews 13:10)

Like Abraham and Sarah and the other people of faith in Hebrews 11, we today have our eyes fixed on that glorious future city that is built by God where we will worship and serve the Lord perfectly forever and ever (11:10). The great cities of this world have no appeal to us, except that they are "great seas" in which to go fishing for souls. Unless we maintain attitudes of transience as we live in this world, we will start to get attached to it, put down our roots and stop living like pilgrims. We start accumulating what Mark Twain called "unnecessary necessities" and forget that our treasures ought to be in heaven. As I mentioned before, Lot committed that sin and lost everything. Our citizenship is on Mount Zion (12:22), our fellowship is with the God of heaven and we aren't ashamed to be pilgrims on this earth.

It's too bad that many Christians think of heaven only when an illness or an accident invades or when death visits and takes a loved one. Heaven isn't simply our destination as pilgrims; it's our motivation for life. Like Moses and the other pilgrims, our values in this life are based on that vision of a glorious eternity. Moses gave up the pleasures and treasures of Egypt because he saw some of the wonders of his future life in heaven, and he bore "disgrace" for the sake of Christ (11:24–27). The apostle Paul had the same experience (Phil. 3:7–14).

Abraham, Isaac and Jacob were wealthy enough to live comfortably in permanent houses, but they chose to live in tents. Why? "For here we do not have an enduring city" (Heb. 13:14), but we do have an eternal city! Wherever Abraham went, there he pitched his tent and built an altar. The tent announced he was a pilgrim and the altar that he was a worshiper of the true and living God. We have an altar, Jesus Christ, through whom we offer our spiritual sacrifices to the Lord (13:15–16). Let's not be ashamed of letting people know it.

What do we have as God's people? Among other blessings, we have a city, an altar, a High Priest (4:14–16) and an anchor (6:13–20). This takes care of our past, present and future.

What a difference that makes!

We Are Worshipers—Let's Bring Our Best to the Lord (Hebrews 13:9–10, 15–21)

As God's people, we must constantly come to the altar to offer our spiritual sacrifices to the Lord. Jesus is the altar; we don't need the temple furniture (Heb. 13:15). Personal worship is important, but so is public corporate worship with the people of God (10:24–25). Public worship is not only a witness that Jesus is alive, but it's also an opportunity for us to encourage and help one another. The Scottish preacher Ian Maclaren wrote, "Be kind, for everyone you meet is fighting a battle."

The importance of worship cannot be overemphasized. Everything we are and do flows out of our worship of the Lord, and this is true of congregations as well as individuals. The church that minimizes worship will have to operate on the best that human nature can supply; but the Lord is seeking worshipers who worship "in spirit and truth" (John 4:23). This kind of worship is possible when the Spirit of God anoints the Word of God in our inner person, enabling us to express true worship to the Lord. Read the first chapter of Malachi and see what God thinks about people who bring Him cheap worship.

We Are All "Works in Progress" (Hebrews 13:20–21)

When the Lord calls us to a task, He equips us to perform it for His glory. He gives us "everything good for doing his will" (13:21). Not only do we do work for the Lord, but in doing it, we experience God working in us, equipping us for the next assignment. Jesus compared doing God's will to eating food (John 4:34) because obedience nourishes the soul.

As we hear the Scriptures read and explained, as we meditate on them personally, as we pray and obey God's will, the Spirit prepares us for what God has prepared for us. "All Scripture is God-breathed and is useful for teaching, rebuking, correcting and training in righteousness, so that the man of God may be thoroughly equipped for every good work" (2 Tim. 3:16–17).

Note that every believer can find in Scripture everything needed for life and service. The Word of God teaches us what is right ("teaching"), rebukes us when we're not right, corrects us so we get right and trains us so we stay right. It's good to attend conferences and classes, but learning about grace isn't the same as growing in grace. Unless we "digest" the truth God gives us from the Word, practice it in daily life and share it with others, what we learn makes no lasting contribution to our spiritual growth.

Some of my readers will remember the pins many Christian young people used to wear that read "PBPWM—GIFWMY." Translation: "Please be patient with me—God isn't finished with me yet." That's good advice for parents, teachers, pastors or anybody trying to help others mature. (Sometimes we need to be patient with ourselves!) Of course, we can use this statement as an excuse: "Give me more time!" The writer of Hebrews anticipated this "delay defense" when he wrote, "In fact, though by this time you ought to be teachers, you need someone to teach you the elementary truths of God's word all over again" (Heb. 5:12). I can't prove it from Scripture, but I'm convinced that we'll learn in heaven the things we should have learned here on earth. Yes, we'll have glorified bodies, but that doesn't mean we'll have perfectly trained minds. We'll enter heaven with the biblical knowledge we had when the summons came—death or the rapture—and we'll keep on learning more about Jesus throughout all eternity.

You can translate Hebrews 13:13, "Let us, then, keep going out to Him outside the camp, bearing the disgrace he bore." If we want to bear witness for Christ, we must also bear reproach with Christ, and the result will be bearing fruit for Christ. So—let's go out!

7

Responsibility—The Heart of the Matter

For the word of God is living and active.
Hebrews 4:12

Someone has said that the heart of almost every personal problem is the problem in the heart, and these many years as a Christian and a minister have made me agree with that statement. King Solomon wrote, "Above all else, guard your heart, for everything you do flows from it" (Prov. 4:23). "Everything you do" is pretty inclusive. It includes our actions and motives, our thoughts and words, our attitudes and plans and much more. Jesus said that good people bring good things out of the good stored up in their heart, and evil people bring evil things out of the evil stored up in their heart (Luke 6:45). The good people are those who have given their hearts to Jesus Christ and hour by hour permit Him to fill their hearts with His Word and His love.

If we desire spiritual improvement in our lives, we must start by letting God change our hearts, and that's what the gospel of God's grace is all about. "This is the covenant I will make with them after that time, says the Lord. I will put my laws in their hearts, and I will write them on their minds. . . . Their sins and lawless acts I will remember no more" (Heb. 10:16–17; see also Jer. 31:33–34). Under the Old Covenant God's law was written on tablets of stone, but under the New Covenant His Word is being written by the Holy Spirit on the hearts of believers.

Paul wrote to the church at Corinth, "You show that you are a letter from Christ, the result of our ministry, written not with ink but with the Spirit of the living God, not on tablets of stone but on tablets of human hearts" (2 Cor. 3:3). A letter from Christ! Could there be any higher privilege? Conversion is a *crisis* experience that brings us into God's family because we have repented of our sins and put our faith in Jesus Christ. But the Christian life is a *process* experience that makes us more like Christ as we relate to Him through the Spirit and the Word. Paul calls this "being transformed into His likeness with ever-increasing glory, which comes from the Lord, who is the Spirit" (2 Cor. 3:18). It's a miracle experience day by day as we allow the Spirit to use the Word in our lives.

When we go outside the camp, what kind of "letter" are we delivering for others to read? Unfortunately, most people don't read the Bible, but they do read the lives of the people who claim to believe the Bible. After all, most people aren't so ignorant that they can't "read" a person with some degree of accuracy. I recall a bit of poetry that I learned in vacation Bible school many years ago.

> You are writing a Gospel, a chapter each day,
> By the deeds that you do and the words that you say.
> Folks read what you write, whether faithful and true.
> Just what is the Gospel according to you?

That isn't great poetry, but it does express a great truth: we should have such a dynamic relationship with Jesus Christ that others will see Him living in us and working through us. Charles Spurgeon said, "May our life be such that it cannot be understood apart from Jesus; take him away and our whole character would become an inexplicable mystery."[1]

Eliminate God from the life of Abraham and all you see is an old man leaving his ancestral home and wandering in the land of Canaan. He has a son by a servant girl, and when the boy is of age, the boy and his mother are both told to get out. Abraham's wife, Sarah, gives birth to a son when she is ninety and Abraham is one hundred. Explain that! When the miracle boy is older, Abraham takes him up a mountain, puts him on an altar and almost kills him. What's that all about? Abraham's nephew Lot and his family become prisoners of war, so Abraham risks his life and rescues them, but he refuses to take any of the spoil. Abraham's life is an enigma until you notice, "And the word of the Lord came to Abraham . . .".

It's impossible to be rightly related to Jesus if we are wrongly related to Scripture.

You can say the same thing about every servant of God in Scripture, including Jesus. Our Lord met the Father early each day and received the word He needed. "He wakens me morning by morning, wakens my ear to listen like one being taught" (Isa. 50:4). Like a faithful soldier, Jesus reported for duty each day, received His orders and went out and obeyed them. His life was controlled by the word of God. "I always do what pleases him [the Father]" (John 8:29).

Guided by the Holy Spirit, five times the writer of Hebrews wrote words of serious admonition to his readers. Some people call these passages "warnings," but the writer called the entire letter "my word of exhortation [encouragement]" (Heb. 13:22). The first three exhortations focus on our relationship to God's Word, for the way we treat the Word of God is the way we treat the Son of God. It's impossible to be rightly related to Jesus if we are wrongly related to Scripture. The last two statements describe the sad consequences that come to the lives of those who ignore or openly defy the Holy Scriptures.

I'm not going to expound each of these admonitions, but I am going to make a few remarks that may assist you in applying the Word to your own life. Please read each exhortation in your Bible in the light of your own Christian experience.

1. Pay Attention to the Word (Hebrews 2:1–4)

If we don't pay attention to the Word of God, we will start drifting like a boat without an anchor, a rudder or a pilot. We should "pay careful attention" when the Word is read and taught publicly and when we read and study it privately. You don't speed-read the Bible. You don't treat the Bible the way you treat any other book. Failure in the Christian life usually begins with carelessly reading the Bible and then not reading it at all. In all the years I've done pastoral counseling with believers, I've learned that spiritual decay invariably begins with a careless lack of discipline in their devotional life. If we don't pay attention to the Bible, we will start to drift, and drifting spiritually leads to a life with no direction. A spiritual drifter lives by chance, not by faith. If you need to be reminded of what the Bible can do for you if you will let it, read Psalm 119.

2. Believe the Word and Obey It (Hebrews 3:7–19)

The writer uses the nation of Israel at Kadesh-Barnea to illustrate his point (Num. 13–14). They heard the command to enter the land and knew that God promised to give them victory, but they didn't believe it. As a result, they rebelled against the Lord, and instead of receiving His blessing, they aroused His anger. The Lord disciplined them by making them march in the wilderness for thirty-eight years until the older generation had died off. We develop hard hearts when we know what God wants us to do but refuse to believe that He will keep His word and give us success. We question the very character of God. Unbelief is a sin of the will, and in God's sight, it is rebellion. Doubt comes from a fearful heart that says, "I cannot believe." But unbelief comes from a stubborn will that says, "I will not believe!" That is a dangerous attitude to cultivate.

3. Be Diligent, Not Sluggish (Hebrews 5:11–6:12)

"We do not want you to become lazy, but to imitate those

who through faith and patience inherit what has been promised" (6:12). The recipients of the letter had become lazy and childish about their Christian walk. If God's people would put as much diligence and hard work into their Bible study, praying and serving as they do their gardening, golfing and watching the stock market, our churches would be filled with mature Christians. Instead, we have religious infants and children. This passage is often quoted to "prove" that Christians can "lose their salvation," but a careful reading shows it teaches just the opposite (6:9–20). According to our Lord's parable of the sower (Matt. 13:1–9, 18–23), if the soil of the heart doesn't produce fruit, the heart has never been changed by the grace of God. The farmer must be diligent to prepare the soil to receive the seed, and we must be diligent to prepare our hearts to receive God's Word. Only then can we bear fruit for the glory of God.

4. Respect the Word, Don't Rebel Against It (Hebrews 10:26–39)

The true believer who knows what the Bible says and yet deliberately keeps on sinning is asking for God's discipline. A casual attitude toward sin and God's discipline is a result of inattention to the Word, a gradual hardening of the heart and a growing dullness of the spiritual senses. The believer who has no respect for God's Word is like a speeding driver who has no respect for the traffic laws or the local police. Repeated willful sinning leads to painful and tragic consequences (remember Lot) and could lead to death (remember Samson). "There is a sin that leads to death" (1 John 5:16; 1 Cor. 11:27–30). We don't see people actually walking on the Son of God, desecrating His blood and insulting the Holy Spirit, but God sees it and it breaks His heart.

My experience has been that the Father lovingly chastens us when we start to rebel, and this ought to bring us to our senses. If it doesn't, He uses stronger measures, but He will not permit us to despise and defy His Word. After all the love God has lavished on us in Christ, how can we even think of rebelling against

Him? "It is a dreadful thing to fall into the hands of the living God" (Heb. 10:31). Charles Spurgeon said, "God does not permit his children to sin successfully."

5. Pursue Holiness, Not Excuses to Sin (Hebrews 12:14–17)

This is the positive side of Christian holiness. "Blessed are those who hunger and thirst for righteousness, for they will be filled" (Matt. 5:6). "Without holiness no one will see the Lord" is a sobering statement (Heb. 12:14). When we trusted Christ, we were justified, which means we were declared righteous in Jesus Christ; but justification must lead to sanctification, a changed life (Rom. 5:1–11; 6:1–14). A righteous standing before God must result in a righteous walk before the world, for our new standing means we have new life. True holiness involves living at peace with people (as much as possible) and being holy in character and conduct before the Lord (Heb. 12:14).

The same grace that saved us will keep us and enable us to live to please God (see 12:15). Esau was a son of Isaac and a member of a "covenant family," but he lived to satisfy his fleshly appetites and had no interest in spiritual things. He had no holy desires in his heart, so he didn't pursue holiness. When he saw his foolish mistakes, he tried to turn things around, but it was too late. The word translated "godless" in verse 16 ("profane," KJV) is related to "threshold" and means "available to be trodden on." The English word comes from the Latin and means "outside the temple, secular." Esau was a "secular" person. He allowed the people of the world to walk on his heart, and the soil became hard so that he could not trust the Lord. His heart was "common property" for anybody who wanted it.

Just as a successful athlete or musician develops healthy habits and gradually does naturally what the coach or teacher commands, so the maturing believer sees Christian responsibility as a privilege, a releasing of their inner potential to God's glory. Obedience isn't a burden, it's a joy; "His commands are not burdensome" (1 John 5:3) because our obedience is motivated by love.

Win or lose, athletes love the challenge of the sport and the thrill of teamwork, and musicians love beautiful music and the privilege of interpreting it for others through their own instruments or voices. This is true of artists and writers, people who design clothes or decorate houses, gardeners and cooks. Skill becomes a natural intuition or habit, and we don't have to be warned or scolded. To love God and the calling He has given us is the secret of a balanced and happy Christian life.

So, what are we waiting for?

Let's go!

Endnotes

Chapter 2

1. Phillip P. Bliss, "Hallelujah! What a Savior!" (1875).
2. William Stringfellow, *Free in Obedience* (New York: Seabury, 2006), 7.
3. Os Guinness, *Dining with the Devil* (Grand Rapids: Baker, 1993), 21.

Chapter 5

1. H.A. Overstreet, *The Mature Mind* (New York: W.W. Norton, 1949), 42.
2. Note that Revelation 7:15, 11:19, 15:5–8 and 16:1 and 17 indicate "sanctuaries" in heaven for special purposes, but they are not identified as places of worship.

Chapter 6

1. A. W. W. Dale, *The Life of R.W. Dale of Birmingham* (London: Hodder & Stoughton, 1905), 318.

Chapter 7

1. Charles Spurgeon, "Behold the Lamb of God" in *The Metropolitan Tabernacle Pulpit*, vol. 33, 565.

Bibliography of Commentaries on Hebrews

The inclusion of a book doesn't imply that I agree with everything in it, but only that it is evangelical in theology and helpful for further study. The exclusion of a book doesn't mean I have rejected it.

Bruce, F.F. *Commentary on the Epistle to the Hebrews*. Grand Rapids: Eerdmans, 1964. This is part of the New International Commentary on the New Testament.

Hewitt, Thomas. *The Epistle to the Hebrews*. Grand Rapids: Eerdmans, 1979. This is part of the Tyndale New Testament Commentaries series. Don't let its brevity fool you; it's very adequate.

Hughes, Philip Edgcumbe. *A Commentary on the Epistle to the Hebrews*. Grand Rapids: Eerdmans, 1977. This is one of my favorites.

Kistermaker, Simon J. *Hebrews*. Grand Rapids: Baker, 1984. This is part of the Baker New Testament Commentary series.

Morris, Leon, Hebrews in Volume 12 of The Expositor's Bible Commentary, edited by Frank E. Gaebelein. Grand Rapids: Zondervan, 1981. This commentary is concise but not inadequate. It's well balanced.

Murray, Andrew, *The Holiest of All: An Exposition of the Epistle to the Hebrews*. London: Nisbet, n.d. While devotional in its approach, this book is both doctrinal and practical.

Sumner, Robert L. *Hebrews: Streams of Living Water*. Raleigh, NC: Biblical Evangelism Press, 2003. The author is an experienced evangelist and capable theologian. It's an excellent bibliography.

This book was produced by CLC Publications. We hope it has been life changing and has given you a fresh experience of God through the work of the Holy Spirit. CLC Publications is an outreach of CLC Ministries International, a global literature mission with work in over fifty countries. If you would like to know more about us or are interested in opportunities to serve with a faith mission, we invite you to contact us at:

CLC Ministries International
PO Box 1449
Fort Washington, PA 19034

Phone: (215) 542-1242
E-mail: orders@clcpublications.com
Website: www.clcpublications.com

READ THE REMARKABLE STORY OF
the founding of
CLC INTERNATIONAL

Leap of Faith

"Any who doubt that Elijah's God still lives ought to read of the money supplied when needed, the stores and houses provided, and the appearance of personnel in answer to prayer." —Moody Monthly

Is it possible that the printing press, the editor's desk, the Christian bookstore and the mail order department can glow with the fast-moving drama of an "Acts of the Apostles"?

Find the answer as you are carried from two people in an upstairs bookroom to a worldwide chain of Christian bookcenters multiplied by nothing but a "shoestring" of faith and by committed, though unlikely, lives.

To order your copy of *Leap of Faith*

You may order by:
Phone: 1-800-659-1240
E-mail: orders@clcpublications.com
Mail: PO Box 1449
Fort Washington, PA 19034

Discount Code:	LGO 650
Reg. Price:	~~$11.99~~
Special Mission Price:	$5.40
Shipping in US:	4.00
You pay:	$9.40

Name: ______________________________

Address: ______________________________

____

Phone: ______________ E-mail: ______________________

Expert Lifemanship

Warren W. Wiersbe & Ken Jenkins

What do we do with life? Sometimes life's crises, or even its predictability, can derail us from the path of God's purpose. He intends, however, that we live to the full. Learning to wait on God for His overcoming strength will enable us to "rise up with wings as eagles, run and not be weary, walk and not faint."

This grand theme is explored in the words of Warren Wiersbe, punctuated by the stunning nature photography of Ken Jenkins. What is created is an appealing invitation to get a new perspective on your existence in this world—and maybe change your life.

ISBN-13: 978-0-87508-988-1

Another Chance at Life

Warren W. Wiersbe

Have you made a mess of your circumstances? Jesus told a story about such a person—and the answer lay in his loving and forgiving father. If you've come to the end of yourself—or simply need a reminder of God's grace and love—this book is for you.

ISBN-10: 0-87508-996-8
ISBN-13: 978-0-87508-996-6

Too Soon to Quit!

Warren W. Wiersbe

Ready to quit? You're not the only one. Flip through the pages of Scripture—you're in good company. Warren Wiersbe unfolds the stories of fifteen Bible characters who struggled just like you, and tells how you can gain the strength to survive—and thrive—when the road gets rocky.

ISBN-10: 1-936143-00-3
ISBN-13: 978-1-936143-00-9

A Passion for Prayer

Tom Elliff

Of all the disciplines of the Christian life, prayer is perhaps the most neglected. Yet Jesus' brief earthly life was permeated with it. *A Passion for Prayer* seeks to help you develop—or deepen—your communion with God. Drawing on personal experience and God's Word, Pastor Tom Elliff shares principles for daily coming before the throne of grace.

ISBN-10: 1-936143-03-8
ISBN-13: 978-1-936143-03-0

Lift Up Your Eyes

Christopher Shaw

"In this challenging book, Christopher points out the limitations and pitfalls of human solutions. . . . He exhorts leaders to look instead to the Source of help and guidance, Jesus Christ. Warmly and realistically, these daily meditations emphasize that only Christ living in you will produce the character necessary for fruitful service."

Luis Palau
World Evangelist

ISBN-13: 978-0-87508-989-8

Living the Christ Life

Compiled by Rebecca English

If you're serious about serving Christ, you've probably noticed how difficult it is to be genuinely holy and fruitful. Living the Christ Life combines gems from classic authors like Amy Carmichael, Andrew Murray and Vance Havner to create a practical daily devotional on living for Christ not in our strength, but in His.

ISBN-10: 0-87508-974-7
ISBN-13: 978-0-87508-974-4

Let Us Draw Near

Andrew Murray

Andrew Murray reveals how knowing the timeless truths of the divinity and humanity of our Lord, His heavenly priesthood and our access to God's presence helps increase out faith and enables us to dwell in God's presence as He intended.

ISBN-10: 0-87508-772-8
ISBN-13: 978-0-87508-772-6